Petty Capitalism
in Spanish America

Dellplain Latin American Studies

Petty Capitalism in Spanish America:
The Pulperos of Puebla, Mexico City,
Caracas, and Buenos Aires
Jay Kinsbruner

This book describes how people of limited means within the Spanish American economy managed to get started and survive as entrepreneurs between 1750 and 1850. Based on ten years of research and a wide variety of primary and secondary sources, Professor Kinsbruner's cross-cultural profile of small retail grocers offers significant insights that contradict many assumptions of dependency theory.

The study considers profits, business longevity, multiple store ownership, the place of women, governmental intervention and support, and the means by which storekeepers obtained credit to acquire inventories. This is an important case study of the roots of capitalism that sheds new light on the history of economic development in Latin America.

Jay Kinsbruner is professor of history at Queens College and at the graduate center of the City University of New York.

DELLPLAIN LATIN AMERICAN STUDIES

PUBLISHED IN COOPERATION
WITH THE DEPARTMENT OF GEOGRAPHY
SYRACUSE UNIVERSITY

EDITOR

David J. Robinson
Syracuse University

EDITORIAL ADVISORY COMMITTEE

William M. Denevan
University of Wisconsin

John H. Galloway
University of Toronto

John Lynch
University of London

Robert McCaa
University of Minnesota

Linda Newson
University of London

EDITORIAL ASSISTANT

Kay Steinmetz

Petty Capitalism in Spanish America

The Pulperos of Puebla, Mexico City, Caracas, and Buenos Aires

Jay Kinsbruner

Dellplain Latin American Studies, No. 21

Westview Press / Boulder and London

Dellplain Latin American Studies

This Westview softcover edition is printed on acid-free paper and bound in softcovers that carry the highest rating of the National Association of State Textbook Administrators, in consultation with the Association of American Publishers and the Book Manufacturers' Institute.

Copyright © 1987 by the Department of Geography, Syracuse University

Published in 1987 in the United States of America by Westview Press, Inc.; Frederick A. Praeger, Publisher; 5500 Central Avenue, Boulder, Colorado 80301

Library of Congress Catalog Card Number: 86-51526
ISBN: 0-8133-7272-0

Composition for this book was provided by the author.
This book was produced without formal editing by the publisher.

Printed and bound in the United States of America

The paper used in this publication meets the requirements of the American National Standard for Permanence of Paper for Printed Library Materials Z39.48-1984.

6   5   4   3   2   1

for Jennifer and Mieca

Contents

Figures

Tables

Preface

This book is a study of small retail grocers and their grocery stores in several Spanish American cities from roughly 1750 to 1850. In examining each city I attempted to discover specific things about the grocers and their stores, but I did not force a predetermined comparative structure upon the documentation. Rather, I permitted the documentation to contribute to an overall picture. The book is a comparative study in that similar matters were explored wherever the documentation allowed.

Many aspects of the public and private lives of the grocers are considered in this book, but my central concern has been to produce a valid economic profile. To do this it was necessary to study the grocers in more than one city. Each city chosen fulfilled a specific need of the project. Puebla was chosen because it was an interior provincial city. Mexico City commanded attention because it was the most populous city in Spanish America, the capital of first a great viceroyalty and subsequently a nation. Caracas was a modestly sized capital city. Buenos Aires was a palpably business-oriented city, one that was far removed from the others studied, and one that was impressive as the capital of a viceroyalty and later a nation. The grocers of San Juan, Puerto Rico, were studied to determine what differences might have prevailed in the Caribbean. Because these were few, I have made only references to San Juan. The grocers of New York City were studied for international perspective, and a discussion of them appears in the conclusion.

Studying the grocers in so many different cities presented innumerable problems. Especially nettlesome was the unevenness of the documentation among the cities. One of the reasons that there have been few cross-cultural historical studies for Spanish America is that it is rarely possible to address precisely the same questions in two countries because the nature of the documentation varies in both quality and quantity. The more countries that are added, or in the present case cities, the more the problem is exacerbated. Thus, in the present instance it was not possible to establish rigid methodological criteria for comparative purposes.

Beyond confronting the large problems of cross-cultural research, there are smaller matters with which to contend. The basic primary sources for this study were censuses, wills, intestate proceedings, company contracts, and litigation. One can be overly confident of the validity of these kinds of documents. Take, for instance, the matter of two lists of store owners for one city, separated in time by a few years. The temptation has been strong for investigators to take such censuses on face value and determine such matters as business longevity, but even a simple and straightforward store census may be fundamentally inaccurate. That is, in many places there were unenumerated partners who appeared as store "owners" on a subsequent store census. This is sometimes the case with partner-wives. In some places this would not be a major problem because of adherence to traditional name forming. But in Mexico the wives frequently employed only their maiden names. In both instances the two censuses really do not demonstrate business longevity or the lack of it. Many stores survived longer than the documents suggest. Further, sometimes store managers were listed as if they were the owners, whether they were invested partners or not. Even when a store was sold the manager may have stayed on and been the one listed in the census.

Other kinds of censuses must be used with discretion. In some places the enumerators employed varying criteria, and this prevailed even within cities and for a single census. Sometimes in a nominal or property census there is what amounts to secondary information that was casually taken and manifestly inaccurate. Some censuses employed the individual's full name; others did not. Even within a single census the practice often varied within a particular city. Thus, Juan Blanco Mello of one part of a city may well be the Juan Blanco (or even the Juan Mello) of a different part of the city. But more troublesome, the Juan Blanco Mello of one city, section, street, or even house in one year may in fact not have been the Juan Blanco Mello of the same location at the same moment, no less some time later. We may be dealing with near relatives of the same name. While this tells us much, it tells far less than some have surmised.

Even that most sanctified of primary documents, the last will and testament, must be used with caution. One person's memory, recorded at a most inauspicious moment in perhaps a long life, was sometimes at odds, understandably enough, with the facts. But even when the will was a precautionary instrument there were sometimes errors. Some testators filed more than one will over the years. Those studying a long time span may be lucky enough to encounter these additional wills (lucky indeed when the wills may have been recorded by different notaries, and the investigator may not have been studying the subsequent notaries). I have seen examples of more accurate factual presentation in a later will, including the mention of previously held property and continuing long-standing debt. The basic character of wills varied regionally. Those of Caracas and San Juan, for instance, were very specific, with the testator often itemizing personal wealth. Mexican wills, on the other hand, often were more general statements.

Further, there was a question of presentation. Earlier manuscript versions of this book ran some 600 pages, with separate chapters dealing with each city studied. Included was a 150-page chapter on the grocers of New York City. Such an approach permitted presentation of a considerable amount of information but at the expense of a systematic discussion of the data. Additionally, since the success of that presentation depended upon consideration of the grocers and their stores according to a series of fundamental questions, repetition became obtrusive. Consequently, I decided upon a thematic presentation, resulting in a much shorter, more easily readable book, but one with its own liabilities. Much material had to be deleted or relegated to simple references in the notes.

From the point of view of research this is a kind of book that James Lockhart warned against in his pioneering *Spanish Peru, 1532-1560*[1]:

> To do the necessary notarial research for a specialized study covering a longer period, such as for example 'Artisans in Colonial Peru,' appears a sheer impossibility, not to speak of the wasted effort that would be involved, scanning so much material which would be irrelevant to the immediate purpose. (And notarial records are not easy to scan.)

Indeed, it took ten years, and the "scanning" of hundreds of interesting documents for every one that proved pertinent to the present project. The result is the first broadly based cross-cultural study of an entrepreneurial, nonartisan group of Spanish American people stationed at the lower end of the socioeconomic scale, a study that because of its scope and detail I think the reader will find convincing.

This book was not written to test an hypothesis; rather its goal is a meaningful picture of the grocers and their stores in an effort to illuminate a critical but obscure transitional period in Spanish American history. Although my interests were very much economic, the book nevertheless is "social history" in our current usage. Like other works of its kind, it does not enjoy the unifying force of a progressively developed argument. What the reader will gain from this book is a sense of what life was like at the very beginning of the entrepreneurial continuum. The "profit gained by the reader of social history," Lockhart perceptively noted, "is more diffuse" than a book of reasoned argument--it is "the feel for a subject matter."[2] This is the logic of the present book.

The dates in this study are a little misleading. There is material on the grocers for all of the period from about 1750 to 1850, but periods emphasized differ among the cities according to the nature of the sources.

---

[1] James Lockhart, *Spanish Peru, 1532-1560* (Madison, pb., 1968), p. 269.

[2] Ibid., p. 221.

Spanish terms have been rendered in English, except where clarity (as in the instance of the Venezuelan *bodega*) suggested the original, or where translation (as in the Mexican *tienda mestiza*--mixed store) would have been awkward. Unless otherwise stated, the terms grocer and grocery store always mean *pulpero* and *pulpería* in this book.

Throughout this book many store values are presented. These values are extremely important to an understanding of grocery stores and other stores as well. Sometimes the values are taken (as noted) from inventories or statements made in wills. Three caveats are in order concerning these values. The first is that in some cases (mostly wills) the store might have had outstanding debts not recognized or noted in the papers. Therefore, the supposed worth of the store might be overstated. Only later appeals or litigation by creditors would demonstrate this. My sense of the documentation used in this book is that this overstatement would have occurred only in a small minority of cases. The second is that retail grocers purchased varying parts of their inventories on credit. This means that in terms of store operation many of the values given in this book are understated--they represent net capitalization values. And finally, the valuations of some stores represent businesses in decline and may not reflect an earlier, or for that matter later, capitalization.

It would be extremely informative to be able to correlate monetary values among the regions, but this is simply impossible in our present state of knowledge. Even when it is possible to discern a uniformity of currency in the Spanish American colonial period we are unable to judge comparative purchase value, and this is the significant value for a cross-cultural analysis. The situation is severely compounded during the national period since currencies often fluctuated widely. The store values presented in this book are significant basically in comparison with others in the same region and with stores in other categories of operation.

Parts of Chapter 3 originally appeared as "The Pulperos of Caracas and San Juan during the First Half of the Nineteenth Century," *Latin American Research Review* 13, no. 1 (1978): 65-85.

Jay Kinsbruner

Acknowledgments

This book originated in an essay that I wrote about capitalism in late eighteenth- and early nineteenth-century Spanish America. Three scholars read the manuscript and offered valuable suggestions. In the order that they read it, they are: Professor Magnus Mörner; Professor Stanley Stein; and Professor Immanuel Wallerstein. I thank all three.

My constant guide--and often inspiration--for the Caracas phase of the project has been Professor John V. Lombardi. To him I owe a great deal and my sincere thanks. In Caracas, Professor Kathy Waldron and Professor Robert Ferry (then both doctoral candidates) were of immense help. Professor Waldron directed me to specific sources. Professor Germán Carrera Damas was kind enough to offer archival advice. Don Leopoldo Méndez, director of the Archivo del Consejo Municipal; Fray Césaro de Armellado, director of the Archivo Arquidiocesano de Caracas; Profesora Ermila Troconís de Veracoechea; the staffs of the Archivo General de la Nación; and the Archivo del Registro Principal de Caracas were all extremely helpful during my two research trips to Caracas.

An orientation in Mexican archives and recent publications was generously provided by Professor Richard Morse. Much general and specific advice was provided by Professor Richard E. Greenleaf. Working one Sunday at INAH alongside Professor Greenleaf, my first graduate teacher 18 years earlier at Mexico City College, was a special pleasure. Professor Linda Arnold guided me through the Mexican archives, directed me to specific sources, and even located, photocopied, and sent me many valuable items. Professor Criston I. Archer and Professor John E. Kicza were both very helpful. Peter Stern helped the project along at a critical juncture. Professor Asunción Lavrin made a timely intervention that helped me gain access to the notary archive of Mexico City. Don Antonio Pompa y Pompa helped me acquire more than 10,000 frames of microfilm for Mexico City and Puebla. I want to acknowledge my great debt to the director and staffs of the Archivo General de la Nación; the Archivo de Notarías del Distrito Federal; the Biblioteca Nacional; the Hemeroteca

Nacional; the Archivo del Ex-Ayuntamiento de la Ciudad de México; the Mormon Reading Room; and INAH, for their extraordinary courtesy and help. The staff of the Archivo del Ayuntamiento de Puebla; the Archivo General de Notarías de Puebla; and the Biblioteca Palofax were all very helpful.

In San Juan the director and staff of the Archivo General de Puerto Rico were most supportive. Professor Thomas Mathews and Dr. José Curet aided the project.

Helpful suggestions for the Buenos Aires phase came from Professor Lyman L. Johnson, Professor Susan M. Socolow, Professor Richard Slatta, and Professor Vera Blinn Reber. The staff of the Archivo General de la Nación was very cooperative, allowing me to consult far more material each day than was customarily permitted.

Two colleagues aided considerably with the New York project. Professor Leo Herskowitz directed me through the archives and pointed out specific collections. Professor William Chute mentioned relevant books and even placed several directly in my hands. I am pleased to acknowledge my great debt to the late Herbert Sakofsky, Esq., for answering my many questions about American legal terms and procedures. The staffs of the Historical Documents Collection at Queens College; the Municipal Archives; the Office of the City Register; the Manuscript Room of the New York Public Library; and the New York Historical Society were all especially helpful. I would like to thank Mr. Robert Towers for arranging for me to have an enlargement of a map of Mexico City of 1811, made from a negative loaned to me by Linda Arnold.

Several colleagues read parts of the manuscript at varying stages of its development and offered significant suggestions. They are: Professors Magnus Mörner, John E. Fagg, John V. Lombardi, John Kicza, Leo Herskowitz, William Chute, Andrew Whiteside, and Jay Gordon. The editor of this series, Professor David Robinson, made many helpful suggestions. I thank them all. Naturally, I alone am responsible for errors.

Finally, I want to thank my wife, Karen, for her supportive editorial assistance.

Funds for the initial phase of the project were provided generously by the PSC-CUNY Faculty Research Award Program.

J. K.

Abbreviations

AAM	*Archivo del Ex-Ayuntamiento de la Ciudad de México* (Mexico City)
AAP	*Archivo del Ayuntamiento de Puebla* (Puebla)
ACM	*Archivo del Consejo Municipal* (Caracas)
AGNA	*Archivo General de la Nación* of Argentina (Buenos Aires)
AGNM	*Archivo General de la Nación* of México (Mexico City)
AGNV	*Archivo General de la Nación* of Venezuela (Caracas)
AGPR	*Archivo General de Puerto Rico* (San Juan)
AHH	*Archivo Histórico de Hacienda* (Mexico City)
AJP	*Archivo Judicial de Puebla* (Puebla)
ANM	*Archivo de Notarías del Distrito Federal* (Mexico City)
ANP	*Archivo de Notarías de Puebla* (Puebla)
BNM	*Biblioteca Nacional de México* (Mexico City)
FA	*Fondos Antiguos*, AJP
HAHR	*Hispanic American Historical Review*
HDC	*Historical Documents Collection*, Queens College

IG	*Indiferente General*, AGNM
IGG	*Indiferente de Guerra*, AGNM
INAH	*Instituto Nacional de Antropología e Historia* (Mexico City)
LARR	*Latin American Research Review*
MA	*Municipal Archives* (New York City)
MC	*Minutes of the Mayor's Court*
MCC	*Minutes of the Common Council of the City of New York*
OCR	*Office of the City Register* (New York City)
Padrón de 1778	Facultad de Filosofía y Letras, Universidad de Buenos Aires, *Documentos para la historia argentina*, tomo XI, *Territorio y Población: Padrón de la ciudad de Buenos Aires (1778)*
PN	*Protocolos Notariales*, AGPR
RP	*Registro Principal* (Caracas)
Recopilación	*Recopilación de Leyes de los Reynos de las Indias*
Tribunales	*Archivo Judicial del Tribunal Superior de Justicia de Distrito Federal* (Mexico City)
Visitas	"Visitas De Tiendas, Bodegas, Pulperías y Platerías, 1799-1809," ACM

1
Basic Characteristics

The small retail grocery stores of Spanish America, the *pulperías*, were largely urban businesses. Their immediate supervisory agency was the town council, which regulated such matters as weights, measures, hours of operation, and what might be sold legally.[1] The grocers who operated these stores, the *pulperos*, comprised the largest group of small, independent entrepreneurial storekeepers officially categorized and supervised in Spanish America during the colonial period and the nineteenth century.

The few pulperías situated in truly rural areas for the most part functioned outside municipal supervision. Tending to sell a broader variety of items, they were more like general stores, and they probably had more of a social significance in their regions than did their urban counterparts. Juan Uslar Pietri suggests what may have been the social position of the rural grocer in Venezuela during the early nineteenth century:

> It is really curious to observe how in our little towns of the interior the *pulpero* plays a social role of the same importance as the priest and the chief political official. He represents a place intermediate between law and religion, that gives him a prestige much more intimate, more comradely.[2]

James R. Scobie makes a similar observation about the pulperías of rural Argentina for the latter half of the nineteenth century:

---

[1]Constantino Bayle, *Los cabildos seculares en la America Española* (Madrid, 1952), pp. 207-23, 461-65. See also C.H. Haring, *The Spanish Empire in America* (New York, 1963), pp. 156, 254.

[2]Juan Uslar Pietri, *Historia de la rebelión popular de 1814* (Caracas, 1972), p. 117.

the country store--the pulpería in Buenos Aires or the
general store in Santa Fe--was rural Argentina's only social
institution.   The pulpería served as provider of
merchandise, purchaser of products, banker, and sole
dispenser of credit. In the isolation of a lonely countryside,
its role as a place of conviviality and a source of
information and news was perhaps as vital as its economic
functions. In many ways, it took the place of the church,
the school, the club, and the plaza, which were
conspicuously absent on the pampas.[3]

Where urban grocery stores were permitted to sell alcoholic drinks, as in
Buenos Aires, a social atmosphere may have developed.[4]

PULPERIA INVENTORIES

The grocers of Puebla and Mexico City sold at retail basic
provisions such as lard, oil, vinegar, rice, and beans, as well as firewood
and charcoal. Wine or hard spirits could not be sold unless the grocers
added a wine store to their operations. Additionally, some grocers retailed
machetes, shovels, cloth, sewing material, chairs, hardware, and bottles.
The Mexican grocers were permitted to sell items of international origin;
one that appears in many inventories is cacao from Venezuela.
The following are some of the items stocked by Don José
Reymundo de Moya in his Mexico City grocery store in 1792.[5] Although
declared a grocery store, the inventory makes it clear that the owner was

---

[3]James R. Scobie, *Revolution on the Pampas: A Social History of
Argentine Wheat, 1860-1910* (Austin, 1964), p. 62. In the early nineteenth
century an Englishman, E.E. Vidal, travelled through parts of Argentina
and later had this to say about the rural pulperías: "The *pulperias* are most
miserable, dirty hovels, where may be bought a little *canna*, or spirit
distilled from the sugar-cane, cigars, salt, onions perhaps, and so near the
city bread, but farther in the interior, this last article is not to be procured;
so that the traveller, unless he carry bread with him, must live, like the
country-people, on beef alone (E.E. Vidal, Esq., *Picturesque Illustrations
of Buenos Ayres and Monte Video*...[London, 1820; reprint ed., Buenos
Aires, 1943], p. 67).

[4]Government officials in Buenos Aires were concerned about the negative
impact of just such an atmosphere (see pp. 90-93).

[5]AHH, Consulado, Leg. 492-6.

also operating a wine store.   There were 154 separate entries for an inventory with a wholesale value of 558 pesos:

firewood	shrimp
charcoal	different kinds of cloth
vinegar	starch
quicksilver	anchovies
hides	ham
beans (many different kinds)	eggs
rice (different kinds)	canes
salt	grain
palm mats	lard
bottles and flasks	honey
glasses	olives
anisette	bread
aguardiente (brandy)	candles
mistela	cheese
wine from Malaga	sugar
chocolate	sacks
empty barrels	*chilito* (an alcoholic drink)

In 1802 Don Juan Monasterio sold a Mexico City grocery store with an inventory valued at 4,268 pesos.[6] The inventory listed 331 separate entries, including many items similar to those in Moya's inventory. This one, however, also contained cacao from both Venezuela and Guayaquil, oregano, garbanzos, corn, nuts, wooden shovels, peppers, and small brushes.

The main wholesale suppliers to the grocers of Mexico City and Puebla were the *tiendas mestizas*, mixed stores that sold food and

[6]AGNM, Consulados, Tomo 160.   Examples of other grocery store inventories in Mexico City are in AHH, Leg. 492-12 (1788); idem., Leg. 684-12 (1811); AGNM, Consulados, Tomo 200, "Inbentarios formados por muerte del Sargento Don Jose Xaraba" (1797) (three inventories); AGNM, Consulados, Tomo 200, "La parte de Don Juan Monasterio con Don Bartolo Alcedo como fiador de su Hermano Don Matias" (1802); ibid. (1805).   Another grocery store inventory may be seen in John E. Kicza, *Colonial Entrepreneurs: Families and Business in Bourbon Mexico City* (Albuquerque, 1983), p. 115. For the town of Zempuala, see AGNM, Consulado, vol. 75 (1809), Valdés vs Padre Francisco de la Concha, Año de 1809. Peter Boyd-Bowman has published the inventories of two country stores in his article, "Two Country Stores in XVIIth Century Mexico," *The Americas* 28, no. 3 (Jan. 1972): 237-51.

hardware items in larger lots than did the small retail grocery stores.[7] In 1787 Don José de Arriaga, a grocer representing his colleagues, petitioned the Puebla town council in search of relief from a 30-peso annual tax newly imposed upon the grocers.[8] Because the grocers had such little capital, he stated, they were forced "to take their goods on credit, and even

---

[7] I have seen no hard evidence that the tiendas mestizas were the main wholesale suppliers to the pulperías in Mexico City, but no other category of store was in a position to act as supplier. On the difference between the two kinds of stores, see the description in the regulations of 1810, BNM, Ms. Division, Ms. 1320, 20 Feb. 1810. The relationship between the two categories of stores is clearer for Puebla. See AAP, Tomo 227, Leg. 2692, ff. 366-76.

[8] AAP, Tomo 227, Leg. 2692, ff. 366-76. In 1788 the royal treasury in Mexico City ordered the merchant tribunal to inform it of the difference between pulperías and *cacahuaterías* on the one hand and tiendas mestizas on the other. In what the tribunal referred to as "*la tierra adentro*," the term pulpería or cacahuatería was unknown. Such designations were used only in Mexico and Veracruz (one should add Puebla also). In the tierra adentro, pulperías or cacahuaterías were called "Tendajos o Tendejones y se distinguen de las demas en que aqui en las Pulperias o Cacahuaterias, esto es, todo lo que se sirve para el alimento, y su preparacion de los vecindarios, semillas, como Aba, garbanzo, etc. Jarcia, y demas cosas de poco valor...." Generally, the tribunal observed, these stores had "principales mui cortas, que apenas dejan a sus dueños lo mui necesario para mantener la vida pobremente aun con respecto a los gastos moderados que se acustumbran en dicha tierra adentro."
  The other stores of the interior were the mestizas, "por que en ella se expenden generos de Europa America, y Assia, quinquilleria, ferreteria, para el Laborio de Haziendas, y Minas y en una palabra todo aquello que tiene consumo en los Lugares en que se cituan...." (AHH, Consulados, Año de 1788, Leg. 696-10, No. 222). The merchant tribunal should have known that there were pulperías in the "tierra adentro" and that the distinction between them and the mestizas in the interior was sometimes blurred in practice. Earlier in the decade it had been observed in a royal document filed in the merchant tribunal archive that "En Guadalajara y las jurisdicciones foraneas de Nueva España respecto de no haber distincion entre las tiendas mestizas y las de Pulperia, satisfagen todos las pensions...." (ibid.). By the turn of the century the *tiendas de cacahuatería* generally became subsumed under the rubric of pulpería.
  Technically, there were two kinds of pulperías: those created by *ordenanza*, that is, a specific number determined by the Crown; and those of *composición*, that is, among a number determined by the local officials. In 1785 the Crown threw open to anyone the choice of opening a pulpería (AHH, Consulados, Leg. 550-90).

at third and fourth hand from the other storekeepers called Mestiza...."[9]
The grocers did purchase some products, he observed, such as bread,
candles, and lard, directly from the producers of these items rather than
from the tiendas mestizas, while they purchased other items such as fruit,
vegetables, and eggs at public market in the plazas.[10]

A fundamental staple in the diet of both poor and affluent was
bread, an item that brought the small retail grocer both profits and
problems. Throughout Spanish America, bread was manufactured by the
wholesale bakers, the *panaderos*. Because of the importance of bread to
the general population and the town council's obligation to guarantee
basic supplies, the price of bread seems always to have been regulated. In
1757 the grocers of Mexico City were permitted a maximum profit of one
real on every peso's worth of bread purchased from the bakers (in this era
the grocer received 16 loaves for a peso).[11] On this basic staple the law

---

[9]Ibid., ff. 370-76. In 1794 the merchant tribunal of Mexico City stated
that to stock their stores the grocers had to find guarantors, and what they
purchased under bond cost them regularly more than what they would
have paid in cash (AGNM, IGG, vol. 60-B, Consulado to Viceroy
Branciforte, 8 Aug. 1794).

[10]Apparently there were also the equivalents of both *regatones* and
pulperías in colonial Brazil. Rae Flory and David Grant Smith in "Bahian
Merchants and Planters in the Seventeenth and Early Eighteenth
Centuries," *HAHR* 58, no. 4 (Nov. 1978): 571-94, speak of "the city's
petty retailers who were largely tavernkeepers and grocers (*vendeiros*) and
street venders (*regateiros*)" (p. 573 n.7). The *vendas* are mentioned also
by A.J.R. Russell-Wood, "Colonial Brazil," in *Neither Slave Nor Free*,
eds. David W. Cohen and Jack P. Green (Baltimore, 1972), pp. 84-133.
Russell-Wood observes that "Possession of a provision store, which
usually doubled as a tavern, offered the maximum financial security and
the highest social position to which the free colored person could aspire.
Municipal registers for the colonial period record single free colored
women and free colored couples possessing not only such stores but one
or two slaves as well....Such vendas sold everything from food, drink,
clothing, and domestic items to firearms, knives, agricultural tools, and
mining bowls '*Bateias*'" (p. 101).

[11]"Ordenanzas para el común de los tenderos de Pulperia...," in published
form in AAM, Tomo 3452, Expediente 2. More recently they have been
published in Fabián de Fonseca y Carlos de Urrutia, *Historia general de
real hacienda*, 6 vols. (Mexico City, 1945-53), 4: 333-72; and Francisco
del Barrio Lorenzot, comp., *Ordenanzas de gremios de la Nueva España*
(Mexico City, 1920), pp. 167-73. See also John C. Super, "Bread and the
Provisioning of Mexico City in the Late Eighteenth Century," *Jahrbuch*

stipulated a maximum profit of 12.5 percent. Those grocers able to sell bread in less time than they had to pay for it would have made a handsome profit over the course of time. However, bread was also a liability. Rioting against high food prices had a long history in Mexico City, and when it occurred the grocery stores were a likely target. There were bread riots in the city following the devaluation of the copper currency in 1837 and 1841, with mobs concentrating their violence on the maize and grocery stores.[12]

The grocery stores of Caracas differed from those in Mexico in two central ways: they were permitted to sell wine and liquor; and they were prohibited from selling items produced outside Venezuela. Actually, there were two categories of small retail grocery stores in Caracas during the period 1750 to 1850, the pulperías and the *bodegas*. A well-known and valuable description of these two kinds of stores was made by the French agent to Caracas, Depons, during the early nineteenth century:

> There are also in Terra-Firma a species of shops known under the name of *bodegas*, and others under that of *pulperias*. Their commodities consist of china ware, pottery, glass, hardware tools, wines, sugar, hams, dried fruits, cheese, tafia, etc. They have an advantage over the other shops, in not being obliged to remain closed on festival days and Sundays. In consequence of their great use and convenience they are allowed to remain open from day break until nine in the evening. This trade is almost exclusively in the hands of active and economical unmarried Catalonians and Canarians; and as it consists in frail and perishable articles, it is liable to damages which must be covered by the profits of its sales; there is not, therefore, an article sold at less than a hundred percent profit, and some often double and treble that amount. It is in this painful and disgusting traffic, that the beginnings of fortunes are much more frequently laid than in any other business.[13]

für die Geschichte von Staat, Wirtschaft und Gesellschaft Lateinamerikas 19 (1982): 159-82.

[12]Frederick John Shaw, Jr., "Poverty and Politics in Mexico City, 1824-1854" (Ph.D. diss., The University of Florida, 1975), p. 334.

[13]F. Depons, *Travels in South America*, 2 vols. (London, 1807; reprint ed., 1970), 2: 74.

Elsewhere Depons observed that the "shops in which inebriating liquors form the basis of their stock, are named pulperias."[14]

Three primary characteristics of the bodegas distinguished them from the pulperías. They sold imported goods, especially nonperishables, including dry goods and wine; their basic trade was not geared to sales of less than a real; and they were typically more highly capitalized than the pulperías.[15]

During the early 1770s the Caracas town council approved an *arancel* for the pulperías of the "Pueblo del Valle de Santa Lucia," a small town over which it held jurisdiction. Among the typical pulpería items listed were:[16]

wine	bacon
aguardiente	lard
syrup from cane juice	sausage
sugar	pork loins
corn	soap
different kinds of bread	firewood
biscuits of wheat	candles
rice	bananas
various kinds of beans	salt
cacao	flour

In 1790 the Caracas town council issued an arancel for the city's bodegas for items such as rice, garbanzos, raisins, nuts, ground cacao, and potatoes, all undoubtedly imported versions of those sold by the pulperías.[17]

By the end of 1804 the merchant tribunal of Caracas (the *consulado*) had won the right of jurisdiction over the *bodegueros*. It was

---

[14]Ibid., p. 116. Frederick P. Bowser has characterized the pulpería in Peru as "something of a small combined grocery store, delicatessen, and tavern." (*The African Slave in Colonial Peru, 1684-1750* [Stanford, 1974], pp. 108-9).

[15]The first two differences are noted in Kathleen Waldron, "A Social History of a Primate City: The Case of Caracas, 1750-1810" (Ph.D. diss., Indiana University, 1977), p. 269.

[16]ACM, Actas de Cabildo, 1773, ff. 21-22, "Arancel que se ha de observar y guardar este Pueblo del Valle de Santa Lucia...." See also Waldron, "Social History," p. 271. No inventories of Caracas pulperías appear to be extant.

[17]AGNV, Capitanía General, Diversos, Tomo 165, "Testimonio de los autos provocados por los bodegueros de esta Ciudad, 1790."

8

not interested in the lowest category of storekeepers, the pulperos, because these dealt only in local items.[18]

The *Almanaque político y de comercio de la ciudad de Buenos Aires para el año de 1826* succinctly defined the Buenos Aires pulperías as "Chandlers Shops in Which Are Retailed Eatables and Liquors."[19] In fact, many grocery stores in Buenos Aires were considerably more like drinking houses than basic suppliers of foodstuffs, although those that maintained a broad inventory sold such items as beans, oranges, starch, rice, sugar, vinegar, yerba maté, pepper, soap, candles, and corn.[20] An Englishman who saw the city's grocery stores during the 1820s observed that they sold every kind of item; they were, he thought actually bazaars.[21] A newspaper advertisement for the sale of a grocery store in 1819 stated that the store stocked grains, skins, salted meat and pork, barreled tongue, and what may have been fresh beef ("*ganado vacuno*").[22] The Buenos Aires grocery stores also sold bread and shoes, items that caused their owners legal problems.

---

[18]"Representación del Prior y Cónsules para que el Tribunal del Consulado se le conserve la jurisdicción...," reprinted in Mercedes M. Alvarez, *El tribunal del real consulado de Caracas*, 2 vols. (Caracas, 1967), 1: 307-11. See also her brief description of bodegueros and pulperos in *Comercio y comerciantes* (Caracas, 1963), pp. 50-51.

[19]The *Almanaque de 1826* was compiled by J.J.M. Blondel and published originally in Buenos Aires in 1825; it was reprinted in Buenos Aires in 1968. This citation is from p. 181. Remembering the period of about 1800-30, José Antonio Wilde wrote: "El *pulpero* no sólo vendía comestibles, vino y toda clase de *bebida blanca*, sino que en invierno despachaba café, que servía en jarritos de lata, con tapa, por la cual pasaba una bombilla también de lata, o a veces de paja" (*Buenos Aires desde setenta años atrás*, 2nd ed. [Buenos Aires, 1948], p. 175).

[20]Three pulpería inventories are in AGNA, Hacienda, X 8-4-3. Two pulpería inventories have been published in Jorge A. Bossio, *Historia de las pulperías* (Buenos Aires, 1972), pp. 229-31 n.32, and pp. 277-79. Bossio's is a wide-ranging account that treats a much broader time period and greater geographical area than my own study. He is intent upon depicting the grocers as a social class, something difficult to confirm. Nonetheless, it is a valuable book with interesting information.

[21]Un Inglés, *Cinco años en Buenos Aires, 1820-1825*, 2nd ed. (Buenos Aires, 1962), p. 114.

[22]*Gaceta de Buenos Aires* (facsimile edition, 1914), 10 March 1819, vol. 5, p. 495.

It was the considerable emphasis on drinking inventory that distinguished the Buenos Aires grocers. In 1815 Doña Ana Correa Morales' small retail grocery store had on hand 7 barrels of aguardiente (either rum or brandy); 28 flasks of local wine; 2 barrels and 4 flasks of pure Malaga wine; 1 barrel and 28 flasks of gin; and some anise or anisette.[23] Don José Seoane had the largest and most highly capitalized pulpería encountered during this study, supposedly valued at 80,000 pesos. Although Seoane denied that his store's capitalization ever reached that figure, the inventory nevertheless displayed a considerable component of alcoholic beverage, reflective of a rather large operation. It included a cask ("*pipa*") of brandy, 5 1/2 casks of wine, 7 barrels of Malaga, plus rum, gin and the like.[24] Doña Sebastiana Fuentes claimed in 1815 to have had the limited capital investment of only 200 pesos, and her store's inventory bears her out. However, although a truly small grocery store, it stocked 18 flasks of ordinary aguardiente and 22 flasks of anise or anisette.[25]

Although local custom and government interference produced regional variation, small retail grocery stores in the cities investigated stocked basically the same items.

THE NUMBER OF GROCERY STORES

Store-to-population ratios differed considerably among the cities investigated. During the late colonial and early national periods Puebla comprised 6 parishes, the most important of which, Catedral, held 47 small retail grocery stores and 45 tiendas mestizas in 1798.[26] The smaller parish of San José supported 22 groceries and 7 tiendas mestizas.[27]

---

[23]AGNA, Hacienda, X 8-4-3, Deposition of Doña Ana Correa Morales, 1 Dec. 1815.

[24]Ibid., Deposition of Don José Seoane (n.d.).

[25]Ibid., Deposition of Doña Sebastiana Fuentes, 20 Nov. 1815. There are many other similar examples.

[26]AJP, FA Roll 41 (microfilm), INAH, "Padron de Pulperías de Puebla...1798-1799." Several of the 47 stores may not have been pulperías. There is also a short list of pulperías for Puebla in 1788 filed in the same source.

[27]Ibid.

Stores in the remaining, less important parishes were not yet referred to as pulperías. Between 19 October 1807 and spring 1808, 158 small retail grocery stores functioned in all of Puebla.[28] By 1816 there were only 137 of them.[29] During this period Puebla was Mexico's second most populous city, with between 50,000 and 60,000 people.[30] Employing an average of 148 small retail grocery stores during the early nineteenth century and a population of 55,000, the store-to-population ratio would have been 1:372.

Mexico City held the fewest grocery stores in comparison to population. In 1781 there were 219 small retail grocery stores in the city.[31] By early 1806 approximately 250 grocery stores functioned.[32] At

---

[28]AJP, FA Roll 41 (microfilm), INAH, Padrón of 1807-1808 (untitled in original). The padrón listed 194 stores, but many either closed before or during the enumeration period or were converted into another category of store, such as a sugar or cotton store.

The Padrón of 1807-1808 was compiled in part to facilitate collection of the alcabala pensión. The *alcabala* was the sales tax. Toward the end of the eighteenth century the Mexican retail grocery stores were required to pay an annual 30-peso *"pensión"* as their entire alcabala assessment. At this time the official alcabala rate in Mexico fluctuated between 3 and 6 percent, at times reaching 8 percent (see Robert S. Smith, "Sales Taxes in New Spain, 1575-1770," *HAHR* 28, no. 1 [Feb. 1948]: 2-37; D.A. Brading, *Miners and Merchants in Bourbon Mexico, 1750-1821* [Cambridge, Eng., 1971], pp. 32-33, 41-42, 60 [n.4]; and J.I. Israel, *Race, Class and Politics in Colonial Mexico, 1610-1670* [Oxford, 1975], pp. 138, 253, 260, 265).

Thus with regard to the small retail grocery stores the 30-peso contribution was often merely a token tax.

[29]AJP, FA, Roll 41 (microfilm), INAH, "Padrón General ó reconocimiento de las Tiendas de Pulperia de esta Ciudad de Puebla..." (1816).

[30]Reinhard Liehr, *Ayuntamiento y oligarquía en Puebla, 1787-1810*, 2 vols., tr. (Mexico City, 1976), 1: 48.

[31]AAM, "Panaderías y Pulperías, 1730-1783," Expediente 33, vol. 1, "Dilix*. q*. conthienen el num*. de Tiendas De Pulpería, Su Cituacion y Dueños de esta Ciudad y Sus Barrios...." As the title indicates, the census includes the city's barrios. Two additional pulperías ceased operations.

[32]AGNM, IG, Unidad: Real Hacienda; Fondo: Reales Cajas; Sección: Real Caja de México, "Padron general de tiendas de esta Capital formado por este Ministerio de Exercito y Real Hacienda para el arreglo del

the beginning of the nineteenth century Mexico City had a population of approximately 137,000 people.[33] Assuming that the city supported some 250 small retail grocery stores at this time, the store-to-population ratio would have been 1:548.

Caracas was similar to Puebla in its store-to-population ratio. The most important group of censuses of grocery stores for Caracas are the *visitas*, the censuses resulting from visits carried out annually by the town council from 1799 to 1809 to check the business practices of various categories of stores.[34] These censuses demonstrate the number of stores operating in the city at the moment of inspection, but there are two basic problems with the resulting counts. One is that they are static and therefore do not indicate store longevity, either prior to the census or after. The second is that the counts may not be accurate. Several of the visitas do not indicate convincingly that specific stores were actually visited and thus were open. When no money was collected for the visit (the storekeeper was required to pay for the supervisory visit) and no fine levied for such infractions as short weighting or not having a license to operate, there is no documentation to prove that a visit to the store actually occurred. Notwithstanding, when the visits were carried out in 1807 and

---

establecimiento del Derecho de Pulperias...." This was a census of all stores in Mexico City and its immediate outlying areas subject to the pulpería tax. A list of grocery stores that had paid the pulpería tax in Mexico City was prepared in 1815 (idem., "Padron gen¹. de las Tiendas de esta Capital por Alfabeto de los Sugetos que las administran. Año de 1815." "Tiendas" is used but clearly refers to pulperías.) Grocers tended to be in arrears, as was the case in 1811 when 58 of them were tardy in their tax payments (idem., Serie: Pulperías, "Lista qᵉ. Comprehende los dueños de Tiendas de Pulperías en esta Corte qᵉ. no han pagado...la Pension..." [1811]). Thus the 1815 census is to be considered incomplete. However, several of the 249 stores listed were no longer functioning pulperías. One was a sugar store; another had become a chocolate store, and two were grain stores. Two pulperías simply did not possess the inventory of the trade. Another was wholesaling. (Many other examples of changes in other categories of storekeeping and of openings and closings of pulperías are to be found in the "visitas" to stores; licenses; and certificates of opening and closing, all in AGNM, IG.)

[33]For the population of Mexico City in the nineteenth century, se⸍ A. Davies, "Tendencias demográficas urbanas durante el sig¹ México," *Historia Mexicana* 21, no. 3 (Feb.-March 1972): 48⸍

[34]Visitas.

1808, Caracas supported 102 operating small retail grocery stores.[35] The following year there were 116 stores in operation at the time of inspection.[36] However, during the course of any of these years, fewer grocery stores actually operated. For instance, in 1809 as a whole, approximately 80 small retail grocery stores functioned in Caracas at any given moment. With a population of 31,473, the city had a store-to-population ratio of 1:393.[37]

The most accurate census of small retail grocery stores in Caracas was that prepared by officials of the royal treasury in 1816.[38] It lists 112 pulpería operations, but this number includes every small retail grocery store that functioned in the city during the course of the year and some of these had closed. However, at any given moment during 1816, Caracas had between 75 and 80 functioning small retail grocery stores in actual operation.[39]

The Caracas store censuses of the early nineteenth century also include the other retail grocery stores, the bodegas. During this period there were approximately 25 percent fewer bodegas in the city than pulperías, although the ratio between the stores fluctuated somewhat according to openings and closings.[40]

---

[35]Visitas. See also Waldron, "Social History," p. 272. The reader may notice that my figures are more conservative than Waldron's. I have not included stores that were, according to the visitas, closed. She apparently has referred only to the sum totals, which include closed stores.

In 1733 the Crown organized the small retail grocery stores of Caracas into two taxed groups: those in the category of ordenanza and those of composición. The ordenanza stores were those whose tax belonged to the city, while the composición were those whose tax belonged to the royal treasury. In 1733 there were 30 ordenanza and 37 composición grocery stores (Waldron, "Social History," p. 278; AGNV, Real Hacienda, La Colonia, "Composición de pulperías, 1717-1765," vol. 2397). By 1760 there were 45 composición grocery stores in the city, while in 1765 there were 44 of them (AGNV, Real Hacienda, La Colonia, "Composición de pulperías, 1717-1765," vol. 2397, ff. 178, 187-88.

[36]Visitas.

[37]Visitas. The population figure is from Waldron, "Social History," p. 28.

[38]AGNV, Real Hacienda, vol. 2423, "Año de 1816, Recept*. Admon de Alcabalas de Caracas, Quaderno de Pulperias."

[39]Several stores remained in business only a few months and are not included in this estimate.

[40]Visitas.

Among the cities investigated, Buenos Aires had the greatest number of grocery stores in relation to population. In 1813 the port city's population was approximately 43,000, and there were 457 small retail grocery stores, rendering a store-to-population ratio of 1:94.[41] By 1824, with a population of approximately 60,000, the city counted 502 small retail grocery stores, a ratio of 1:120.[42] These high store-to-population ratios may have been reflected in the very modest capitalizations of a majority of the city's small retail grocery stores in 1813 (Table 9).

FEMALE GROCERS

Historians no longer accept the traditional view that women were economically inactive during the colonial period and the early nineteenth century. There were indeed legal and social restrictions set against women, the most disabling being the colonial Spanish injunction

---

[41]Enrique M. Barba, in *Almanaque político y de comercio de la ciudad de Buenos Aires para el año de 1826* (Buenos Aires, 1968), pp. xv-xvi, for the population figure; and AGNA, Hacienda, X 8-4-3, "Arreglo y Razon de la Contribucion extraordinaria que se señala a los gremios de almaceneros, Fabricantes De Belas y Marquetas de Sebo, Jaboneros, Pulperos y Boticarios de esta Capital...Agosto de 1813," for the number of stores. According to García Belsunce, there were at least 364 pulperos in the city in 1810 (César A. García Belsunce [Director], *Buenos Aires; su gente, 1800-1830* [Buenos Aires, 1976], p. 118). Johnson and Socolow ("Population and Space in Eighteenth Century Buenos Aires," in *Social Fabric and Spatial Structure in Colonial Latin America*, ed. David J. Robinson [Ann Arbor, 1979], p. 351) estimated the number to be 428. Both of these figures are derived from the census of 1810, for which several *cuarteles* are missing. Of the 364 pulperos estimated by García Belsunce, 70.6 percent were "españoles--europeos," with 54.6 percent having migrated from Galicia. Sixty-six pulperos were porteños, presumably from the port itself (p. 119). For the limitations of the 1810 census, see García Belsunce, *Buenos Aires*, pp. 61-66, and Johnson and Socolow, "Population and Space," pp. 339-68. García Belsunce (*Buenos Aires*, p. 118) uses the figure 558 for the number of "pulperos" in 1813. I have settled upon the figure 457 and the term "pulpería." (There were 392 pulperías in Buenos Aires in 1793. Bossio has published a census of pulperías for that year [Appendix 7, pp. 281-306]).

[42]*Almanaque de 1826*, pp. xv, 181-99. There are errors in the *Almanaque*; I have calculated 502 stores.

14

prohibiting married women from entering into contractual arrangements without permission from their husbands.[43] Yet some women managed to be not only active but entrepreneurial.

There were urban centers where women were well represented among the grocers. For instance, in Santiago, Chile during the 1760s it appears that most grocers were female, "from the dregs of the population, *zambas*, Indians and Mulatas...."[44] There were 38 pulperías in the town of Paucartambo, Peru in 1824, and all were run by women.[45]

Nevertheless, in the cities considered in this study women were decidedly underrepresented. In 1789 there were 6 female grocers, either owners or managers, in Puebla's Catedral parish, comprising only 12.8 percent of the total.[46] In 1807-1808 Puebla had approximately two dozen female grocers among its 158 small retail grocery stores, still only a modest 15 percent of the total.[47] By 1816 the number of female grocers had declined by more than half. Now there were 137 stores but only 10 female owners or managers, down to 7.3 percent.[48]

In Mexico City in 1781 women owned 11 percent of the small retail grocery stores (1 woman owned 2 of them).[49] Among the nearly

---

[43]This law was modified somewhat in the nineteenth century for the colonies that remained within the empire. Asunción Lavrin has summarized the legal position of women in *Latin American Women: Historical Perspectives*, ed. Lavrin (Westport, CT, 1978), pp. 30-31. For an excellent discussion of women in the colonial economy see Colin M. MacLachlan and Jaime E. Rodriguez O., *The Forging of the Cosmic Race* (Berkeley, 1980), pp. 236-48.

[44]José Toribio Medina, ed., *Cosas de la colonia* (Santiago, 1952), pp. 88-90.

[45]Magnus Mörner, "La distribución de ingresos en un distrito Andino en los años 1830," Research Paper Series, Paper no. 1, January 1977, Institute of Latin American Studies, Stockholm, p. 13.

[46]AJP, FA, Roll 41 (microfilm), INAH, "Padron de Pulperías de Puebla...1798-1799."

[47]Ibid., Padrón of 1807-1808.

[48]Ibid., "Padrón General ó reconocimiento de las Tiendas de Pulperia de esta Ciudad de Puebla..." (1816).

[49]AAM, Expediente 33, vol. 1, "Panaderías y Pulperías, 1730-1783," "Dilix". q°. conthienen el num°. de Tiendas De Pulpería, Su Cituacion y Dueños en esta Ciudad y Sus Barrios...." In 1806, 16 grocery stores were

240 small retail grocery stores current in their tax payments in 1815 there were only 13 female owners (several may have been administrators rather than owners).[50]

Women were even more underrepresented among the small retail grocers of Buenos Aires. In 1778 the city had 194 small retail grocers, with only 1, or perhaps 2, women among them.[51] According to a census of 1813, there were only 19 female owners of small retail grocery stores.[52] It is possible that some of the men listed in the census were only administrators for female owners or that some male owners had female partners. However, perhaps 1 or 2 of the women listed were actually administrators for male owners. All possibilities considered, there were still few female owners, comprising approximately 4 percent of the total. In 1825 only 23 out of the city's 502 small retail grocery stores were owned by women, a slightly higher percentage than in 1813.[53]

What is also noteworthy about female store ownership in Buenos Aires is that in 1813 not a single female grocer owned a store capitalized at more than 3,000 pesos, a fairly modest amount when one considers that many men owned more heavily capitalized ventures. While only about 51 percent of the male owners owned stores capitalized under 501 pesos,

---

owned by women (one being in partnership with a man). Estimating 269 pulperías and tiendas mestizas paying the pulpería tax, there would have been less than 6 percent female ownership (AGNM, IG; Unidad: Real Hacienda; Fondo: Reales Cajas; Sección: Real Caja de México, "Padron general de tiendas de esta Capital formado por este Ministerio de Exercito y Real Hacienda para el arreglo del establecimiento del Derecho de Pulperias...compiled 1806).

[50]AGNM, IG; Unidad: Real Hacienda; Fondo: Reales Cajas; Sección: Real Caja de México, "Padron gen¹. de las Tiendas de Esta Capital por Alfabeto de los Sugetos que las administran. Año de 1815."

[51]Padrón de 1778.

[52]AGNA, Hacienda, X 8-4-3, "Arreglo y Razon de la Contribucion extraordinaria que se señala a los gremios de Almaceneros, Fabricantes De Belas y Marquetas de Sebo, Jaboneros, Pulperos y Boticarios de esta Capital...Agosto de 1813."

[53]*Almanaque de 1826*, pp. 181-98. These calculations are my own. As noted, there are errors in the *Almanaque*, and sometimes full names are not given. A list of stores and *almacenes* (wholesale-retail operations) compiled in 1802 noted only two female owners (García Belsunce, *Buenos Aires*, p. 127). García Belsunce also observes that the important census of 1810 notes only one female storeowner--but this should be considered a further indication of that census' inadequacies.

almost 74 percent of the women owned stores capitalized this modestly (Figure 1).[54]

Caracas also had few female grocers (Appendix 2). A partial census of the pulperías in Caracas for 1760 lists 45 stores and not a single female grocer. The same is true of the 44 stores listed for 1765.[55] Of the 116 pulperías listed in the visita of 1809, not one appears to have been owned by a woman.[56] Nor does there appear to have been a woman owner of any of the city's 85 bodegas of 1809.[57] However, again, visitas may have recorded an administrator's name rather than the owner's. Rarely were partners listed, and some of these may have been women.

One of the interesting female grocers of Caracas was Doña Josefa Guevara, born in nearby Petare. Doña Josefa married a Spaniard, and they had a son. After her husband's death, she married again. This time she had a daughter, but the child died at three. From her first marriage she had inherited a coffee hacienda that functioned on rented lands. With the hacienda she inherited 7 slaves, 18 mules, a house and the like. But the earthquake of 1812 and the disasters of the wars of independence left her with nothing. During her second marriage she acquired with her husband and "with our industry" one-half of a pulpería in Caracas. Doña Josefa made it clear in her will that the pulpería had been acquired through her efforts also and was part of her estate.[58]

---

[54]AGNA, Hacienda, X 8-4-3, "Arreglo y Razon de la Contribucion extraordinaria que se señala a los gremios de Almaceneros, Fabricantes De Belas y Marquetas de Sebo, Jaboneros, Pulperos y Boticarios de esta Capital...Agosto de 1813."

[55]AGNV, Real Hacienda, La Colonia, vol. 2397, "Composición de pulperías, 1717-1765."

[56]Visitas.

[57]Ibid.

[58]RP, Escribanías, 1817 (Castillo), ff. 11-12, Will of Doña Josefa Guevara, 18 Feb. 1817. Names within parentheses for RP and ANM notes are the notaries.

17

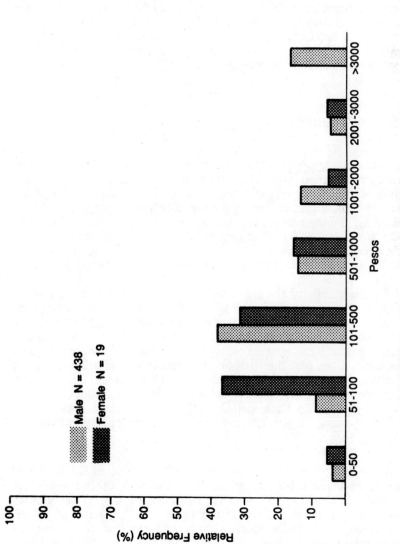

Figure 1. A Comparison of Capitalizations of Male-Owned and Female-Owned Grocery Stores in Buenos Aires in 1813.

18

Doña Josefa was not unique in her exactitude of mind and awareness of personal property within a marriage. In Mexico Doña María Antonia de Figueroa y Marmolejo, daughter of a notary, owned a grocery store "in company" with her husband. Neither had brought anything of value to their marriage, but when Doña María wrote her will in 1786, she and her husband owned the store that they had purchased "with money acquired by us both...." Therefore, she noted, one-half of the profits belonged to her. Further, she was also an equal partner with her husband in a "little house" constructed at their expense.[59]

SPATIAL DISTRIBUTION

It is not always possible to determine a store's precise location. For instance, location was sometimes recorded as a corner without indication of which side of the street. Thus a store situated over a period of years at a particular corner may have changed its physical location several times. Furthermore, there rarely exists a coincidence of accurate map and store location information, limiting the possibility of charting location over long periods of time. It has been possible, nevertheless, to map store locations for three of the cities, albeit at particular moments.

By the middle of the eighteenth century, street names in Puebla, especially those close to the center of the city, generally ran for only one block, making it possible to determine store location with greater accuracy than when street names ran across several blocks. However, street names in Puebla frequently changed according to the name of the current leading local resident. Even near the business, governmental, and religious center of the city, street names periodically changed. One example among many was Calle del Colegio de Ynfantes, which in 1754 was called Calle de la Aduana Vieja, in 1785 Calle del Colegio de los Infantes, and in 1826 Calle de la Aduana Vieja o Infantes. After independence, the names of

[59]ANM, (Adán), vol. 1784-1787, ff. 194-197, Will of Doña María Antonia de Figueroa y Marmolejo, 12 Sept. 1786. Another pulpera was Doña María Félix Morales, who in 1810 owned a Caracas grocery administered by her husband (RP, Escribanías, 1800 [Texada], ff. 29-32, Will of Doña María Félix Morales). For an example of a woman's becoming the principal owner of a bodega through inheritance and then perpetuating the commercial cycle, see ibid., 1813 (Castillo), ff. 41-43, Hidalgo-Viera contract, 1 April 1813. For an excellent account of the life of a female *pulque* dealer, see Edith Couturier, "Micaela Angela Carrillo: Widow and Pulque Dealer," in *Struggle & Survival in Colonial America*, eds. David G. Sweet and Gary B. Nash (Berkeley, 1981), pp. 362-75.

streets and plazas were occasionally altered to express new symbolic meanings.

The center of public activity in Puebla, as in other Spanish American cities, was the main plaza.[60] The plaza had three arcades, the most important in the city: the Portal de la Audiencia, the Portal de Borja, and the Portal de las Flores. In 1798 the Portal de la Audiencia had two stores, both of them tiendas mestizas. On the other side of the plaza and closer to the cathedral was the Portal de Borja (which in 1852 became the Portal de Iturbide); in 1798 it held six tiendas mestizas and one sugar store. The third of the plaza's arcades, near the public fountain, was the Portal de las Flores (in 1852 renamed the Portal de Morelos); in 1798 this arcade held three tiendas mestizas.[61] At the end of the eighteenth century the main plaza contained no pulperías, but this was soon to change.

Several of the city's important streets, each a single block long and radiating from the plaza, also were without small retail grocery stores. Calle de los Herreros was during the late eighteenth century one of Puebla's principal streets.[62] In 1798 Herreros supported two tiendas mestizas and one sugar store. Calle de la Santísima had two tiendas mestizas and a sugar store. Calle de Guevara had a tienda mestiza and a small food and china store. One of the most important streets was Calle

---

[60]For an interesting discussion of the historical role of the main plaza, see Daniel W. Gade, "The Latin American Central Plaza as a Functional Space," in *Latin America: Search for Geographic Explanations*, ed. Robert J. Tata (Chapel Hill, 1976), pp. 16-23. A vivid description of a market day in 1849 is in Guillermo Prieto, *Ocho días en Puebla* (Mexico City, 1944), pp. 104-6. For a description of the public market in 1823, see W. Bullock, *Six Months' Residence and Travels in Mexico...*" (1824; reissued, Port Washington, NY, 1971), pp. 104-6. Valuable background information on Puebla is to be found in Jan Bazant, "Evolución de la industria textil poblana (1544-1845)," *Historia Mexicana* 13, no. 4 (April-June 1964): 473-516; and idem, "Industria algodonero poblana de 1800-1843 en numeros," *Historia Mexicana* 14, no. 1 (July-Sept. 1964): 131-43. See also Manuel de Flon, "Noticias estadísticas de la intendencia de Puebla," in *Relaciones estadísticas de Nueva España de principios del siglo XIX*, ed. Jesús Silva Herzog, *Archivo Histórico de Hacienda*, vol. 3 (Mexico City, 1944), pp. 52-54.

[61]Information on number of stores from AJP, FA Roll 41 (microfilm), INAH, "Padron de Pulperías de Puebla...1798-1799"; information on the plaza from Hugo Leicht, *Las calles de Puebla: estudio histórico* (Puebla, 1934), pp. 337-41, and passim.

[62]Leicht, *Las calles de Puebla*, p. 212. For an excellent description of the streets and finer homes of Puebla in 1823, see Bullock, *Six Months' Residence*, pp. 83-86.

20

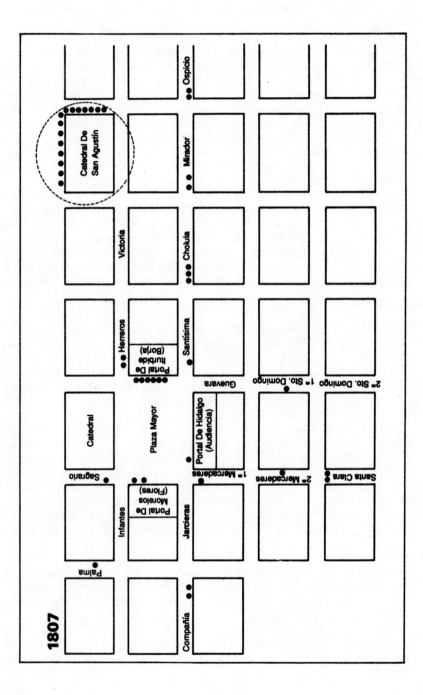

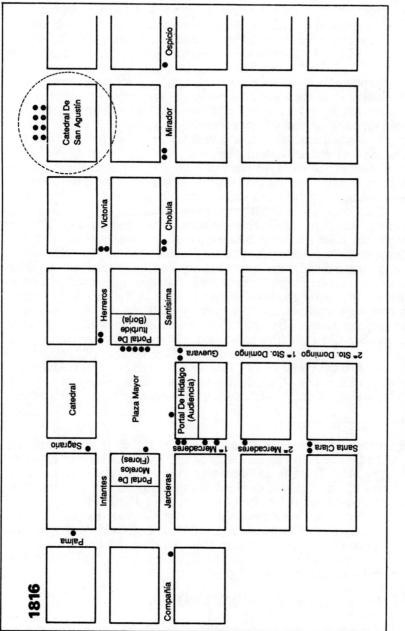

Figure 2. The Small Retail Grocery Stores of Several Streets near Puebla's Plaza Mayor in 1807 and 1816.

de los Mercaderes, often referred to as Calle 1ª de Mercaderes because the succeeding street, which had the same name, was called Calle 2ª de Mercaderes. In 1798 Calle 1ª de Mercaderes had two tiendas mestizas and one sugar store. On 2ª de Mercaderes there were also two tiendas mestizas and one sugar store. Calle Victoria was the next street following Herreros. In 1798 it had two tiendas mestizas, one grocery store, and one "Tienda."[63]

Surprisingly, there were no small retail grocery stores in the main plaza at the end of the eighteenth century. Two blocks away from the plaza may not have been significant when it came to profits, but the distance suggests the status of grocery store ownership in Puebla's scheme of things. Since there was a clear difference between grocery stores and tiendas mestizas in Puebla during this era, and since Catedral parish held 47 of the former and 45 of the latter in 1798, some branch of government must have induced this distribution. It is doubtful that a free market economy would have produced such a spatial arrangement.

The local government was more interested in licensing and controlling the basic retail grocery stores than the tiendas mestizas; consequently, more and better information exists about the former. It has not been possible to determine the total number of tiendas mestizas in Puebla during the early nineteenth century nor their locations. In 1807 there were six grocery stores in the Portal de Borja, one in the Portal de la Audiencia, and two in the Portal de las Flores.[64] Thus, Puebla's central plaza now supported nine grocery stores were there had been none only ten or so years earlier. By 1807 Calle de los Herreros had two grocery stores and Santísima one (two had closed). There was now a grocery store at the corner of the plaza and Mercaderes and one on 2ª de Mercaderes.

In 1816 the Portal de Borja housed five grocery stores, Audiencia one, and las Flores one. Calle de los Herreros held two, Guevara two, and 1ª de Mercaderes four.[65] Thus, during the early nineteenth century there

---

[63]Information on number of stores from AJP, FA, Roll 41 (microfilm), INAH, "Padron de Pulperías de Puebla...1798-1799"; Leicht, *Las calles de Puebla*, p. 241. There is an interesting point about Catedral parish in 1798: on Calle de Yglesias there existed the pulpería of the "Padre Don Francisco Cuebas" (AJP, FA, Roll 41 [microfilm], INAH, "Padron...1798-1799"). Churchmen were prohibited by the Laws of the Indies from operating pulperías (*Recopilación*, 1: 124). For a priest's progressive views on commerce, see Fray Juan Villa Sánchez, *Puebla: Sagrada y Profana* (Puebla, 1835; reprint ed., Mexico City, 1962), p. 41. Sánchez actually made his statement in 1746.

[64]AJP, FA, Roll 41 (microfilm), INAH, Padrón of 1807-1808.

[65]Ibid., "Padrón General ó reconocimiento de las Tiendas de Pulperia de esta Ciudad de Puebla..." (1816).

were small retail grocery stores in and near the main plaza, as well as elsewhere (Figure 2).

Two essential characteristics of Spanish American streets during this period are significant to a consideration of small storekeeping. First, the streets radiating from the central plaza in many cities, including Puebla, were very long. A small retail grocery store at one end of the street might very well seem an eternity away from one at the other end, or even the middle, when it came to attracting or losing customers. Further, a relative isolation would be enforced during the rainy seasons, when mud made streets almost impassable. Second, many more people lived on these streets than one might think. During the late eighteenth and early nineteenth centuries, Puebla was so heavily populated that it may be presumed that some blocks in the vicinity of the main plaza housed several thousand people. Some streets, including opposite corners, could have easily supported four, six, or eight retail grocery stores.

In fact, it was not unusual for potentially competing stores to cluster, as in the case of Mexico City (Figure 3).[66] While many streets were not serviced by small retail grocery stores in Mexico City in 1806, others supported two, three, or more grocery operations (Figure 3). The concentration of small retail grocery stores in or near the main plaza is particularly noteworthy. The small street of the Portales de las Flores (Figure 3, Letter A) contained 5 grocery operations. The little area of Calle de Flamencos and the Plazuela Volador (Figure 3, Letter B) held 14

---

[66]Employing a well-known map of 1811, it has been possible to locate 178 small retail grocery stores that were in operation in 1806 (AGNM, IG; Unidad: Real Hacienda; Fondo: Reales Cajas; Sección: Real Caja de México, "Padron general de tiendas de esta Capital formado por este Ministerio de Exercito y Real Hacienda para el arreglo del estableciemento del Derecho de pulperias..." [compiled 1806]). Many stores that could not be located were in the outer areas of the city. About two dozen other stores either had closed or altered their categorical status by January 1806. All of the stores listed in the census of 1806 and placed on the map functioned as grocery stores, although some indeterminate number were also tiendas mestizas. However, these were few in number; that is, most of the stores were fundamentally grocery operations. Other censuses and general information about the grocery stores and the tiendas mestizas suggest that there would have been approximately 250 grocery stores operating in Mexico City at any given moment during the early nineteenth century, not including stores that were basically or exclusively tiendas mestizas.

Well-known descriptions of market life in Mexico City are in Antonio García Cubas, *El libro de mis recuerdos* (Mexico City, 1945), pp. 219, 238-39; and Fanny Calderón de la Barca, *Life in Mexico*, ed. Howard T. Fisher and Marian Hall Fisher (New York, 1970), p. 110.

24

of these small stores. The street Bajos de Portaceli (Figure 3, Letter C) supported 9 grocery operations. The Calle de Meleros had 6 grocery stores, and just off Meleros was the Calle del Colegio de Santos (Figure 3, Letter D), which in early 1806 supported 10 grocery stores. That is, just in this one area were nearly 50 grocery operations, more if other streets near the main plaza were included.

Like Puebla in the late eighteenth century, Caracas in the early nineteenth century lacked pulperías in the most important commercial center of the city, the main plaza, although 9 bodegas were situated there (Figure 4).[67] Further, there were at least 12 additional bodegas in the plaza's immediate vicinity. Interesting also is that bodegas were located in groups in several parts of the city. At minimum, 10 corners and streets held at least 3 bodegas. One street had 7 bodegas, and 1 supported 5 of these grocery stores. There was no legislation or official attempt to cluster the bodegueros.

The location of the pulperías away from the commercial center of the city was not a response to natural market forces but rather a response to governmental interference.[68] Both the town council and the governor desired the main plaza to be the central market for the residents of Caracas. This would contribute to order, easy supervision, and tax collection.[69] Around 3 sides of the plaza were about 45 canastillas (fixed shopstalls), which opened into the plaza. These measured 8 feet by 8 feet each. Within the plaza itself were small wooden huts, called ranchos, which sold food products. In 1788 there were 67 ranchos and 45

---

[67]Figure 4 depicts most of Caracas in the early nineteenth century, and virtually all of the old city, radiating from the main plaza. The map was prepared from an excellent one of 1843. On it were placed the pulperías of 1808 and the bodegas of 1809. There were 102 pulperías in operation at the time of the 1808 visita, and it was possible to place 66 of them on the map (visitas). The remaining 36 could not be located, but most of them were in the outlying districts. Eighty-two bodegas were in operation during the 1809 visita, and it was possible to place 64 of them on the map (ibid.).

[68]Through the use of the visitas, it has been possible to verify such absence for several other years during the early nineteenth century. As the map demonstrates, there were only two pulperías in close proximity to the main commercial plaza and market, and even if there were one or two others from among the stores not located, the total would be surprisingly few.

[69]Waldron, "Social History," pp. 260-61.

canastillas at the main plaza.[70] The municipal government desired to gather as many dry goods and food sellers at the main plaza as possible. In addition to fulfilling one of its central obligations, that of insuring a steady and reasonably priced food supply for the city, the town council stood to reap a considerable financial reward. The municipal government owned the canastillas and ranchos at the plaza. The rent for the canastillas was 4 1/2 pesos per month, plus a 5-peso monthly sales tax. Rents for the ranchos seem to have been determined according to the product sold (and probably the size of the rancho). At one point a rancho that sold fresh fish paid 3 pesos a month; one that sold bread paid 2 pesos; and one that sold fruit paid 8 1/2 pesos a month.[71] By the 1780s the municipality had elevated the plaza into the city's main marketplace for fish, dairy products, meat, vegetables, and fruit. Over the next decades about 40 percent of the municipal government's total income derived from the rents at the plaza.[72]

Altogether, retail store rents became critical to the functioning of the municipal government, far more important than the interests of the pulperos. It is not clear whether the municipal government would have permitted pulperos to locate in or near the main plaza, or would have thwarted such efforts. What is certain, however, is that the municipal government contrived to have the main plaza offer many of the same items ordinarily stocked by pulperías.

A final point of interest is that unlike those of Mexico City, the Caracas pulperías rarely clustered. With the exception of the main commercial district, the pulperías were located throughout the city, and except in isolated instances, tended to be located at least a block or street away from each other.

---

[70]Ibid., pp. 261-62.

[71]Ibid., p. 262.

[72]Ibid., p. 264. The municipality also rented bodegas in the main plaza. During the late eighteenth century many pulperos also rented store space from the town council but probably not in buildings near the main plaza (ACM, Libro de Propios, 1801-1806).

26

Clearly several factors affected the spatial distribution of the small retail grocery stores, and the forces of the market economy were not always paramount. The municipality of Caracas was not the only government that attempted to regulate store location. In 1757 regulations governing the grocery stores of Mexico City permitted such stores to be established at any street corner but not at mid-block.[73] Those located at mid-block were to be closed. The restriction was probably unsuccessful since it had to be repeated in a decree of 1764. In 1785 an order signed by José de Gálvez suspended the decree and permitted the grocers to establish their stores wherever they chose.[74]

[73]AAM, Expediente 2, Tomo 3452; Fonseca and Urrutia, *Historia general*, 4: 332-72; Lorenzot, *Ordenanzas de gremios*, pp. 167-73.

[74]AHH, Consulados, Leg. 696-10, no. 222, Año de 1788.

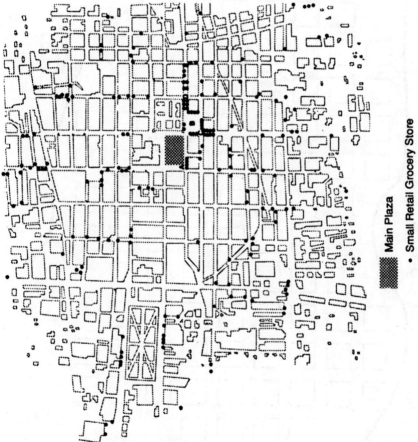

Main Plaza

• Small Retail Grocery Store

Figure 3. Small Retail Grocery Stores in Mexico City in 1806.

28

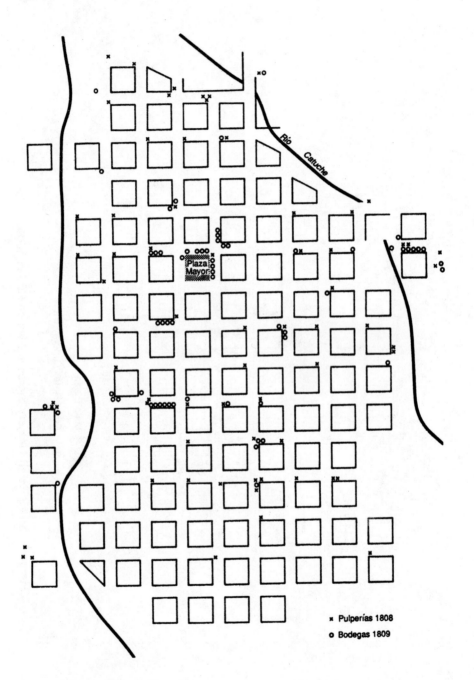

Figure 4. Pulperías and Bodegas in Caracas in 1808 and 1809.

2
The Grocers as Entrepreneurs

The grocers organized businesses at risk for profit; that is, they were entrepreneurs. For their efforts they have not enjoyed a very fine reputation. Recall that Depons thought the grocers were involved in a "painfull and disgusting traffic...."[1] In his petition to the town council of Puebla in 1787 on behalf of the grocers, Don José de Arriaga described problems inherent in grocery store operation that caused tardy payments to creditors. Thus the grocers lost their honor; they were referred to as "Thieves, Swindlers, etc...."[2] Reminiscing about Buenos Aires in the early nineteenth century, José Antonio Wilde wrote that the majority of the grocers, while not quite from the bottom rank, were men who, in general, had very little learning.[3] Recently the distinguished Chilean historian, Mario Góngora, gauged the grocers' place in society when he surveyed the merchants down to the *tratantes*, "who were dedicated to short-distance trade in the produce of the land." These "were men of little significance--hardly greater than that of grocers and innkeepers."[4] In her excellent book dealing with the merchants of Buenos Aires, 1778-1810, Susan Socolow described the city's street peddlers, called *mercachifles* or *mercaderes de bándola*. "They were among the poorest and least prestigious groups engaged in commerce...Of approximately the same social ranking were the *pulperos*...."[5]

---

[1]Depons, *Travels in South America*, 2: 74.

[2]AAP, Leg. 2692, Tomo 227, ff. 366-76.

[3]Wilde, *Buenos Aires*, p. 175.

[4]Mario Góngora, "Urban Social Stratification in Colonial Chile," *HAHR* 55, no. 3 (Aug. 1975): 421-28.

[5]Susan M. Socolow, *The Merchants of Buenos Aires, 1778-1810* (Cambridge, Eng., 1978), pp. 108-9.

Considering this reputation it is interesting that some grocers enjoyed a relatively greater social standing. Don José María de Torres y Cataño exemplifies the willingness of people of prominence to invest in small retail grocery stores. A lawyer attached to the royal audiencia, this gentleman owned a grocery store in Mexico City in 1810.[6] John Kicza has noted that people high up the commercial hierarchy in Mexico City invested in grocery stores: "wholesalers of the city were quite willing to acquire small neighborhood grocery stores...."[7] Don Manuel Villegas was both the owner of a grocery store and an alcalde of one of Puebla's 16 barrios.[8] Don Ignacio Fuentes of Puebla was an investor in tiendas mestizas, a grocer, and by 1838, a wealthy landowner.[9]

Because of the prestige associated with membership in the militia and regular army, it is significant that some grocers were military officers.[10] In 1807-1808 a grocery store in Puebla was owned by Lieutenant Colonel Don José Segundo López Cordero, and managed by a clerk. The owner was an officer in the regular army.[11] Another store was owned by Colonel Don Ignacio Maneiro, a career officer in the Provincial Infantry of Puebla. Maneiro also had someone managing his store.[12] Don Gabriel Bringas owned two Puebla grocery stores in 1807, and in

---

[6]AGNM, Consulado, Expediente 10, Tomo 164, "Don Manuel Alvarez de Palacios con El Lic^do. D. José María de Torres y Cataño...."

[7]Kicza, *Colonial Entrepreneurs*, p. 233. I have not seen any examples of this but Kicza has seen about a dozen instances and considers the practice common (personal communication from Professor Kicza, 30 August 1981).

[8]AJP, FA Roll 41 (microfilm), INAH, Padrón of 1807-1808.

[9]AJP, FA, Roll 26 (microfilm), INAH, Puebla, 1833-1838, "Testamentaria de Don Ignacio Fuentes."

[10]Christon I. Archer, *The Army in Bourbon Mexico, 1760-1810* (Albuquerque, 1977), passim.

[11]AJP, FA, Roll 41 (microfilm), INAH, Padrón of 1807-1808. Also, Archer, *Army in Bourbon Mexico*, p. 196. Don José Segundo López Cordero was a Lieutenant Colonel in the regular army (personal communication from Professor Archer, 9 May 1979).

[12]AJP, FA, Roll 41 (microfilm), INAH, Padrón of 1807-1808; Archer, *Army in Bourbon Mexico*, p. 196.

1810 he was a captain of militia and an interim commander of the Infantry Batallion.[13]

In Caracas at least one socially prominent individual invested in a grocery store, although this one was a small bodega. Don Simón de Ugarte, born in Spain, resident of Caracas during the late colonial period, was a man of considerable merchant wealth and political influence.[14] At the time of his marriage, his capital was worth, by his estimate, 70,000 pesos. His wife brought no wealth to the marriage but eventually inherited about 1,700 pesos. After his marriage Ugarte's wealth had increased, he thought, "considerably," but during the wars of independence much of it was confiscated by the patriots. During a self-imposed exile he inherited a large amount of money from his brother, who had been his partner. When the wartime situation in Venezuela stabilized with the patriots ascendant, Ugarte returned to Caracas and bought a cacao and coffee hacienda for 40,800 pesos. He also became a partner in a bodega. The partnership in this small store included his brother-in-law and his son-in-law. Ugarte, through the management of his son, invested 1,500 pesos; his brother-in-law invested another 1,500 pesos; and the son-in-law, charged with the "principal work and direction" of the store, invested an additional 1,000 pesos.[15] Surely Ugarte would not have involved his family in such a minor business if it meant jeopardizing their social standing. Whatever else Ugarte and his son may have been, they were now retail grocers.

Another Caracas merchant of substantial reputation who became a grocer was Don Bernardo López Penelas. Born in Galicia, Spain, López (according to his will) had been decorated by the King. He migrated to San Juan, Puerto Rico, apparently during the independence movement. By 1828 he owned a dry goods store in San Juan's main plaza. Previously he had owned a similar store in the same venue. Later he owned another dry goods store, the three businesses having been partnerships that endured only briefly. López also owned a grocery store in San Juan, again in partnership. Withdrawing funds from this store, he opened a second grocery in partnership next to the first one.[16]

---

[13]AAP, Roll 47 (microfilm), INAH, Libro 79, 1810, "Libros del Ayuntamiento de la Ciudad de Puebla." Some pulperos were militia soldiers in Puebla as they were in other cities.

[14]For his political career, see *Actas del cabildo de Caracas, 1810-1811* (Caracas, 1971), 1: passim.

[15]RP, Escribanías, 1835 (Felipe Hernández Guerra), ff. 251-56, Will of Don Simón de Ugarte.

[16]AGPR, PN, Caja 443, ffs. 287-96. In her husband's absence and later death, Doña María de la Concepción Hernández de Penelas, also from

32

Significantly, some grocers were affluent enough to have moved up to more prestigious endeavors. The brothers Giraldes of Buenos Aires are an example. In 1814 the bachelor Don Tomás Giraldes, from Galicia, owned four grocery stores. The year before, one of them was capitalized at 8,000 pesos and a second at 30,000 pesos.[17] To place these figures in perspective one should consider that in 1813 a majority of the grocery stores in Buenos Aires were capitalized at under 501 pesos. In 1813 Tomás' brother Francisco owned a grocery store capitalized at 36,000 pesos.[18] In 1825 the third brother, Nicolas, owned five grocery stores.[19] This brother married the daughter of Don Ignacio Ximenez, who in 1813 owned three grocery stores.[20] Certainly this was not a typical grocer family, but its activities suggest the range of success possible to people who, from the point of view of large wholesale merchants, were just small storekeepers.[21] Some grocers could have moved easily into the lower or

---

Caracas, attempted to continue the San Juan business operations (Ibid., Caja 474, ff. 388-91).

[17]AGNA, Registro de Escribano 4 (Iranzuaga), 1814, ff. 152-53, Will of Don Tomás Giraldes, 5 July 1814.

[18]AGNA, Hacienda, X 8-4-3, "Arreglo y Razon de la Contribucion extraordinaria que se señala a los gremios de Almaceneros, Fabricantes De Belas y Marquetas de Sebo, Jaboneros, Pulperos y Boticarios de esta Capital...Agosto de 1813."

[19]*Almanaque de 1826.*

[20]AGNA, Hacienda, X 8-4-3, "Arreglo y Razon de la Contribucion extraordinaria...a los gremios de Pulperos...Agosto de 1813." Pulpero families elsewhere were sometimes tied through marriage. Antonia Vega y Falcón, from the Canary Islands, married Antonio Hernández, also a Canarian, and both migrated to Puerto Rico in 1818. By 1828 the husband had died and Doña Antonia had five living children (three others had died in infancy). Sons José and Antonio had established a pulpería with capital they had put together themselves. Doña Antonia and her husband had suffered economic reverses and could not help their children financially. Daughter María married Matías Margenal, who owned two pulperías. Daughter Francisca married Juan Canobas, also soon to own two pulperías. That is, this family controlled five San Juan pulperías (AGPR, PN, Caja 443, ff. 376-78).

[21]Examples of failures are in AGNA, Registro de Escribano 4 (Iranzuaga), 1813, ff. 1v-6, Will of Don Ygnacio Ximenez, 5 Jan. 1813; 1815, ff. 153v-155, Will of Don José Benito Roman, 28 June 1815. Many storekeepers attributed their failures to the British invasion of 1806 and

even middle range of import-export wholesaling, the most prestigious of business endeavors.

CREDIT

From the Giraldes extreme to that of the most modest grocer, credit was central to the operation. More than 200 years ago Daniel Defoe judged its importance to the storekeeper: "Credit, next to real stock, is the foundation, the life and soul of business in a private tradesman; it is his prosperity; it is his support in the substance of his whole trade...."[22] Further, he understood that credit expanded the storekeeper's capacity for trade beyond his capital investment: "Hence it is that we frequently find tradesmen carrying on a prodigious trade with but a middling stock of their own, the rest being all managed by the force of their credit."[23]

In 1787 Don José de Arriaga, the grocers' advocate, presented a clear statement about credit in Puebla: the grocers were regularly behind in the payments to their creditors, he stated, to

---

the unsuccessful British attempt the following year. On the British period see Bossio, *Historia de las pulperías*, pp. 82-83.

[22]Daniel Defoe, *The Complete English Tradesman*, 2 vols. (New York, 1970), 1: 269. The book was first published in 1726.

[23]Ibid., 1: 271. For an overview of credit in earlier European trade see Fernand Braudel, *The Wheels of Commerce, Civilization and Capitalism, 15th-18th Century*, vol. 2, tr. (New York, 1982), pp. 73-75, 385. For a general introduction to credit see Adam Szaszdi, "Credit--Without Banking--in Early Nineteenth Century Puerto Rico," *The Americas* 19, no. 2 (Oct. 1962): 149-71. The most important lenders in Spanish America during the period 1750 to 1850 were the Church and the larger merchants. The role of the Church as a lender is well known. In 1966, María Eugenia Horvitz Vásquez, in an excellent thesis, "Ensayo sobre el crédito en Chile colonial" (Memoria De Prueba, unpublished, Santiago, 1966), demonstrated the great extent to which merchants were indeed lenders in the Santiago-Valparaíso region. A brief review of current literature that acknowledges the merchants as lenders is in Arnold J. Bauer, "The Church in the Economy of Spanish America: *Censos* and *Depósitos* in the Eighteenth and Nineteenth Centuries," *HAHR* 63, no. 4 (Nov. 1983): 707-33.

the Baker for Bread; the Candlemaker for Candles; the owner of the tienda mestiza for inventory items; the Pork dealer for Lard, and soap; and the Houseowner, for the rent of the House....[24]

Credit was available for the purchase of the store itself. In 1807 two Puebla grocery stores were purchased for 1,509 pesos, with terms calling for payment of 40 pesos per month.[25] That is, the new owner was given three years to pay off the purchase of two stores. As was customary, the purchaser was required to produce a legal guarantor for his financial obligation. Often the guarantor was another storekeeper whose wealth was considered by all parties to be sufficient to cover the guarantee on the loan. In 1799 a Puebla grocery store was purchased for 853 pesos on the basis of payments of 15 pesos per month; the purchaser put up a house as security.[26]

Sometimes it was necessary to obtain relatively large amounts of capital or goods. In 1807 the administrator of a Puebla grocery store borrowed 127 pesos worth of goods for his inventory, to be paid off at the rate of 5 pesos per week for the first 4 weeks and 6 pesos per week thereafter until satisfaction of the debt. The administrator backed the loan personally and through the use of the store as collateral.[27]

---

[24]AAP, Leg. 2692, Tomo 227, ff. 366-76.

[25]ANP, Notary #6, Leg. 1811, "Expediente promovido por Don José Dominguez como Apoderado de Don José Monte Alvª. de Don José Ygnacio Sarte, contra Don Leonardo Mora Sobre pª." In the litigation over payment the stores were referred to as tiendas mestizas, but this was apparently an error. The civil and criminal litigations for this period housed in the ANP are in bundles tied by cord and marked, often precariously, by a little piece of paper or cardboard with a date and notary number on it. However, the legajos might have several notaries represented within them, and each expediente may involve more than one notary.

[26]ANP, Notary #5, vol. 1800, ff. 2v-4.

[27]ANP, Notary #6, Leg. 1809, "Sobre pª. pʳ. D.J. Ygnº. Marin contra Bernardo Hernandez." An example of credit in another store category illuminates small storekeeping in general. In 1793 María Salazar had a shopstall in Puebla's main plaza for the purpose of "buying and selling shoes." She requested of Doña Micaela López, who also had a shopstall in the main plaza, 200 pesos with which to purchase items for her inventory. López advanced the money under the condition that the borrower would operate her own business but pay López one-half the profits. This was really "not what is understood to be a legal loan, but an

Terms of sale were also attractive in Mexico City. For instance, in 1788 Don José Rincón y Ordaz purchased a grocery store for 1,216 pesos.[28] No initial payment was required; rather the purchaser agreed to pay the seller 40 pesos per month. In the succeeding 22 months, Don José, according to his will of 1789, did not miss a payment.[29] This was a felicitous way to enter a business. If Don José paid out the 480 pesos each year from profits and still had something for himself, his store certainly was profitable.

In 1788 Don Manuel de los Rios purchased a Mexico City grocery store, which he had been administering, for 111 pesos, to be paid off at the rate of 10 pesos per month.[30] Thus an administrator was able to buy a truly small retail grocery store without initial funding on his part.

Not surprisingly, the purchase of a store might portend complications. Don Juan Capelo bought a Mexico City grocery store, which included a wine store operation, in 1842 for 1,451 pesos, to be paid off in six months, not a particularly generous arrangement. The store itself was placed as collateral.[31] Several months after Don Manuel Arce

---

administrative arrangement...." Actually, López had become a silent partner. The borrower was not permitted to secure further loans without López's express consent. Later that year, López advanced another 200 pesos, but under even more stringent conditions. Salazar was required to place in her stall a person approved by López to look after the latter's interests. Profits between Salazar and López were to be divided in half, and an accounting had to be prepared each night. From the profits, López was to be paid a part of her now 400-peso investment. An interesting aspect of this business relationship between two women with stalls in the main plaza is that both sold shoes. Whether or not their shoes were similar in quality and cost, López was clearly displaying a sophisticated sense of business acumen (idem., Notary #5, vol. 1790-1795, ff. 150-52, 270).

[28]ANM, (Adán), vol. 1789, ff. 255-57, Will of Don José Rincón y Ordaz, 19 Dec. 1789.

[29]Ibid.

[30]AHH, Consulados, Leg. 492-12, Sale of the pulpería of Doña María Ynes de Estrada to Don Manuel de los Rios. In 1794 Don José Reymundo de Moya sold a pulpería in Mexico City for 1,000 pesos, requiring no cash down and only a 5 percent interest payment, payable at monthly intervals, for the first year (ibid., Leg. 496-6, 491-68).

[31]Tribunales, Papeles Sueltos, N. 2672, "D. Cristoval Mateos por D. Manuel Arce sobre que D. Juan Capelo le subrogue con otro el fiador que le dió para el pago de una tienda."

sold his store to Capelo he had received news that the affairs of Capelo's guarantor were not in a good state. With confidence lost in the guarantor, Arce attempted to force Capelo to obtain a new one. First he appealed to Capelo but was rebuffed. Then he appealed to the *Tribunal Mercantil*, the Consulado having been abolished. The tribunal ruled against Arce on the grounds that he had agreed to Capelo's guarantor, and no arrangements had been made to allow Arce the privilege of approving or disapproving the guarantor during the life of the contract.[32]

The seller of a store might also find it difficult to collect his money. In 1837 two men bought a store in Mexico City, the nature of which has not been determined, for 787 pesos on the basis of a 100-peso down payment, the remainder to be paid off at the rate of 20 pesos per month. The pair were personally responsible for the debt, and as special collateral they put up the store, which they promised not to sell nor encumber in any way until the debt was paid. In a matter of months the seller was having trouble collecting the debt. "In vain I have exhorted Pacheco a thousand times to comply with his word..." the seller stated. Pacheco was now operating the store by himself (perhaps in management); at one point he fled. The seller appealed to the authorities for permission to take possession of the store in order to regain the money owed him.[33]

The death of a store's purchaser might breach a sale. In the early 1830s Don Tomás Ruíz sold a combined grocery and wine store in Mexico City to Don José María de los Rios. By 1834 Rios had died, still owing the estate of the now deceased Ruíz thousands of pesos. By this date the store was run down, and a committee of creditors was formed to arrange the sale of the business and the meeting of obligations.[34]

Another potential source of funds was the family. In 1770 Don Angel Ruíz borrowed 800 pesos from his wife's sister in order to stock his Mexico City grocery store. The loan was to be paid back over five years at 5 percent interest.[35] But the funding of a small store might also be

[32]Ibid.

[33]Tribunales, Papeles Sueltos, N. 2672, 1837, "Espediente ejecutibo seguido por D. Ygnacio Arroyo contra D. Antonio Pacheco sobre pesos."

[34]Tribunales, Papeles Sueltos, Juzgado de Letras, Año-1834, "Los Acreedores a la testam*. del finado D. Tomas Ruiz...."

[35]ANM, (Adán), vol. 1773, ff. 28-31, Will of Don Angel Ruiz, 20 June 1773. A normal loan was a *depósito irregular*. An especially interesting loan arrangement occurred in the 1780s. Doña María Ygnacia Carrión, a widow, stocked a pulpería with some 400 pesos that she had borrowed from her brother, the priest Don Francisco Carrión. The store was located

burdened by family. Don Juan Maximiano Mena owned a half-interest in a Caracas bodega in 1803. He had contributed 400 pesos of the capitalization, and his two sons had provided the remaining 400 pesos. The husband of his youngest daughter owed someone 50 pesos, and Don Juan had guaranteed payment. Finally, Don Juan was required to pay the debt, withdrawing funds from the bodega to do so.[36]

The documentation for Caracas and Buenos Aires is not so rich with regard to the financial details of store sales, although there were sales, especially in Caracas. During the course of 1816 there were 112 different pulpería operations in Caracas, several succeeding others in the same venue.[37] In this single year two venues had between them nine different pulpería operations. Several stores closed during the year. Twenty-four stores were bought and not resold. It is possible only to estimate the length of time that a purchased store was held prior to resale. However, those stores purchased and resold in 1816 were held between one and six months. Six stores were held less than four months.

The single most important source of funding for commercial and agricultural endeavors during the period under consideration was the Church, yet there is little evidence that the grocers relied on its loans. Of the hundreds of wills examined for this investigation, only one mentioned

---

in a building owned by the priest. It was administered by Don Juan de Ayllón, who was required to give Doña María six reales daily for her and her family's maintenance. At the end of the first two months an inventory was taken and it was discovered that the principal had declined by 46 pesos. However, it was felt that in the future profits would be realized. Thus, after an additional two months, another inventory was taken; this time the principal had declined by nearly 200 pesos. Ayllón had to leave his position, but he offered to make restitution (probably for half the loss) in several ways, including giving up one-third of any future salaries, even in other stores (ANM, [Adán], vol. 1784-1786, ff. 90-91, Loan contract of Ayllón and Carrión, 25 June 1785). He had no other wealth. John Kicza has found many cases of owners suing their former employees for funds. "Many cajeros left their posts in debt and found themselves legally hounded to make repayment, even though they personally owned little property and earned only a meager income (Kicza, Colonial Entrepreneurs, pp. 138-39). Ayllón does not seem to have been hounded, at least for the moment; in fact, he seems to have been entirely correct in his dealings with his employer.

[36]RP, Escribanías, 1803 (Aramburu), ff. 114-18, Will of Don Juan Maximiano Mena, 15 March 1803.

[37]AGNV, Real Hacienda, vol. 2423, "Año de 1816, Recept*. Admon de Alcabalas de Caracas, Quaderno de Pulperias."

a grocer's debt to the Church.[38] The leading student of Church loans in Caracas during this period has not found a single instance of a Church loan to any storekeeper.[39] However, there remains the possibility that some grocers were able to negotiate loans from the Church, as Michael P. Costeloe's description of the personal loans granted by the Church in Mexico suggests:

> By the eighteenth century the ecclesiastical corporations were investing their funds by giving loans at interest to any person who required them, provided that the borrower could furnish an adequate security. Any person could request the loan of a sum of money for a term of five to nine years during which he would pay 5 percent interest on the debt, and at the end of which he in theory was obliged to redeem the capital. In practice an extension at the end of the first term was almost always given. There was no restriction placed on the borrower as to the use which he made of the money, and the size of the loan depended entirely on the amount of funds which were available at the time.[40]

However, there was a problem: "In most cases the only acceptable security was real estate."[41] This restriction naturally would eliminate most small retail storekeepers from the Church's loaning process, but some grocers owned houses and could have used them as security. Not only the landed rich borrowed from the Church; so too did merchants. "Furthermore, it is of interest to note that the small businessman or merchant, from whom liberals might expect to gain support, was frequently seeking loans from the Church."[42] Were small retail grocers among them?

Various Church agencies made loans. Diocesan funds were loaned out by the *Juzgado de Capellanías*. Other Church entities, such as

---

[38] ANM, (Adán), vol. 1772-1774, ff. 2-5, Will of Don Bernardo de Paz y Ulloa, 5 Jan. 1773.

[39] Conversation with Professor Ermila Troconís Veracoechea, Caracas, 2 July 1980.

[40] Michael P. Costeloe, *Church Wealth in Mexico: A Study of the 'Juzgado De Capellanías' In the Archbishopric of Mexico 1800-1856* (Cambridge, Eng., 1967), p. 27.

[41] Ibid.

[42] Ibid.

the regular orders and the colleges, loaned out money on their own, usually at 6 percent interest, a less attractive rate than that of the Juzgado. At times, the loans of these and other ecclesiastical corporations were administered by the Juzgado.[43] Costeloe is properly enthused with the enormity of this banking operation, its effectiveness, influence, and professional expertise. He has concluded that "to the aspiring merchant or impecunious landowner, there was no other source from which funds could be borrowed on easy terms. The *Juzgado* in effect exercised a monopoly in the availability of investment capital."[44] Clearly this was not the case when it came to the small retail grocers. There were other sources of investment capital open to them.

The amount of money loaned by the Juzgado was usually about 4,000 pesos, but this depended upon the amount of liquid capital available to the Church at any moment, limited sometimes by many appeals for loans.[45] The Juzgado rarely took an interest in the purpose of the loan; what counted was "the value of the security and the ability of the prospective borrower to pay the stipulated interest."[46] At times, personal guarantees were permitted as security for a loan.[47] The small retail grocer would not seem a likely candidate for a Church loan.

In fact, through its legacy program the Church sometimes drew funds out of the commercial cycle. Don Pedro Cunqueiro owned a small retail grocery store in Mexico City. Through his will in 1779 he bequeathed his estate to a convent.[48] There were many instances of bequests to the Church from grocers, especially the more affluent ones, although the Church was not named the testator's universal heir. At the level of the small retail grocer the Church probably withdrew more capital than it ever placed in circulation.

----

[43]Ibid., p. 80.

[44]Ibid., p. 29.

[45]Ibid., pp. 66-67.

[46]Ibid., pp. 67-68.

[47]Ibid., pp. 76-78.

[48]ANM, (Adán), vol. 1778-1780, ff. 27-29, Will of Don Pedro Cunqueiro, 29 March 1799. This will has been filed improperly.

BUSINESS LONGEVITY

Essential to an estimation of the grocers as entrepreneurs is the question of business longevity. Were the grocers able to sustain themselves in business long enough to acquire sufficient funds for retirement, for upward movement to a more prestigious category of store, or perhaps for removal to a farm? Further, were the grocers capable of remaining in business long enough to develop skills that would assist them in other ventures? In his 1787 petition to the Puebla town council, Don José de Arriaga observed that since it was necessary for the grocers to leave their stores "in search of daily inventory purchases," it was mandatory to have someone run the store during these absences. Sometimes "we have our women and children whom we can place in charge of the store...."[49] Was there enough business longevity for their children to acquire skills that would enlarge their opportunities? Although the answers to these questions cannot be predicated on a particular number of years of business operation, the fact is that very few small retail grocers managed to remain in business for more than a few years. Nor did their heirs do much better.

Arriaga placed a fine point on this: "...many manage to sustain a store of this kind only a year."[50] In 1794 the merchant tribunal of Mexico City observed to the viceroy that among the owners of grocery and wine stores were few who stayed in business for many months.[51] Yet some grocers survived both the capriciousness of the marketplace and government interference and remained in business for more than just a few months or a few years.

This was certainly the case in Puebla. Between fall 1807 and spring 1808, a total of 158 grocery stores were open in Puebla. Approximately 50 of the owners manifested significant longevity, that is, either the original owner or heirs operated a store for more than just a few years.[52] By 1807 one store had been in business some 40 years, and was

---

[49]AAP, Leg. 2692, Tomo 227, ff. 366-76. On the availability of schooling for children of the lower classes, see Shaw, "Poverty and Politics in Mexico City," pp. 210-22, 407-8. For an overview of education in the period, see Dorothy Tanck Estrada, *La educación ilustrada (1786-1836)* (Mexico City, 1977), passim.

[50]AAP, Leg. 2692, Tomo 227, ff. 366-76.

[51]AGNM, IGG, vol. 60-B, Consulado to Viceroy Branciforte, 8 Aug. 1794. It should be noted that the merchant tribunal was attempting to make a self-serving point in this somewhat hyperbolic communication.

[52]AJP, FA Roll 41 (microfilm), INAH, Padrón of 1807-1808.

then being run by the son of the original owner. Of the 137 small retail grocery stores operating in Puebla in 1816, approximately one-quarter of the owners (or managers) had been in business in 1807 (Table 1). Several had been in business 10 or so years earlier.[53] This longevity is all the more impressive considering the detrimental impact of warfare and epidemic disease during these years.[54] However, longevity did not always convey prosperity. In 1808, for example, the widow Doña María Dávila owned a grocery store at the corner of San Juan de Dios, a store which she had also owned in 1798. Her husband had been the store's owner in 1789. In 1807 Doña María was so impoverished that the intendant relieved her of the tax requirement.[55]

During the early nineteenth century only a small percentage of the grocers of Mexico City remained in business over a long period of time. Thirty-eight grocery stores that had been in operation in 1806 were still

[53]AJP, FA Roll 41 (microfilm), INAH, "Padrón General ó reconocimiento de las Tiendas de Pulperia de esta Ciudad de Puebla..." (1816).

[54]In 1835 Don Francisco de la Peña published Fray Juan Villa Sánchez's 1746 report to the town council on conditions in Puebla. De la Peña, a native of Puebla and an alcalde in 1832 and 1834, appended informative notes of his own. Speaking of the Hidalgo "Insurreccion," he observed that "this City was one of those that most felt its lamentable consequences...." From thirteen to fourteen thousand men left the city as troop re-emplacements. "The epidemic of 1813 carried off more than twenty thousand souls...." Indeed, although the "Actas" of a town council often did not indicate the extent and nature of its daily activities (for instance, those of the alcaldes, *fiel ejecutor*, and *síndico*), the Actas of the Puebla council during the early nineteenth century devote so much space to matters concerning the militia and epidemics that it would appear that little else occupied the attention of the councilmen when they met as a group. De la Peña was an emotional reporter, and even though his figures may be questionable, it is certain that thousands of people lost their lives to disease during the early nineteenth century (Fray Juan Villa Sánchez, *Puebla: Sagrada y Profana* [Puebla, 1835; reprint ed., Mexico City, 1962], p. 105).

[55]AJP, FA, Roll 41 (microfilm), INAH, Padrón of 1807-1808. However, since she did not possess a license to operate the store, the intendant fined her 50 pesos (ibid.).

Table 1

PUEBLA'S GROCERY STORE OWNERS OR MANAGERS OF 1816
WHO WERE IN BUSINESS OTHER YEARS

	Store #	Name	Location	Location Earlier Years	In Business Earlier years
1.	2	Don Gregorio Otero	Portal de Borja	Same	1807
2.	3	Don Juan Solar	Portal de la Audiencia	Same	1807
3.	7	Don Vicente Echavarrí	Calle de Guevara	Different	1807
4.	8	Don Sebastián Ochoa	Calle de la Compañía	Same	1807 (1794, 1798[1])
5.	9	Doña María Quemf	Esq. del Sagrario	Same	1807
6.	16	Don Ygnacio Rosales	Esq. de Peñas	Same	1807 (adm'r)
7.	18	Don José María Campos	Esq. de Victoria	Probably the same	1807 (1798)
8.	19	Don José María Campos	Esq. de Victoria	Probably the same	1807[2] (1798)
9.	24	Don José Marín	San Agustín	Same	1807[3] (1798)
10.	25	Don José Fernandez Cordova	Costado de San Agustín	Same	1807
11.(?)	27	Don José Pinzón	Esq. del Pitihua	Different	1807[4]
12.	30	Don Mariano Oropeza[5]	Cruz de Piedra	Different	1807
13.	35	Don Diego Aranda	Esq. Santa Teresa	Same	1807 (1798[6])
14.	37	Don José Carmón	Calle de Mercaderes	Same	1807 (1798[7])
15.	38	Don Mariano Salas	Calle de las Cruzes	Same	1807[8]
16.	40	Don José Larrasilla	Alguacil Mayor	Same	1798
17.	42	Don José María Valle	Plaza de San Francisco	Probably the same	1807
18.(?)	48	Don José Flores[9]	Esq. Santa Rosa	Different	1807
19.(?)	51	Don Francisco Truxillo[10]	Esq. San Roque	Different	1807
20.	64	Don Félix Ramiro	San José	Different	1807
21.(?)	67	Don Miguel Carrera	2ª de San Luis	Different	1807

22.	70	Don Matías Muñoz	Recogidas	Same	1807
23.	76	Don Joaquín Fortis	Tepetlapa	Same	1807[13]
24.	79	Don José Ortiz	Portal del Alto	Same	1807
25.	85	Don Manuel Villegas	Cascabeles	Same	1807 (1789[14], 1799)
26.	87	Don Ygnacio Acevedo[15]	Esq. de la Tesorera	Same	1807
27.	88	Don Manuel Oropeza	2ª de Mercaderes	Same	1807
28.	93	Don Francisco Nieto	Nahuala	Same	1807
29.	97	Don Ygnacio Lopez	Torreblanca	Different	1807[16]
30.	100	Don José Marzoa	Calle de Belen	Different	1807
31.(?)	101	Don Francisco Vargas	Portal de Borja	Different	1807[17]
32.	111	Don Cayetano Carmón	1ª de Mercaderes	Different	1807
33.	112	Don Carlos Alvarado	Real de San José	Same	1807
34.	113	Don Manuel Arcos	Esq. del Hospicio	Same	1807
35.	115	Don Juan Azcarate	Esq. de Herreros	Different	1807 (sold a pulpería)

Notes

1. Store 8 was an azucarería in 1794 and 1798. 2. One of Campos' stores was a tienda mestiza in 1798. 3. Marín owned a cacahuatería in 1788. 4. The name for 1807 is Don José María Pinzón. 5. He is listed for store 62 also in 1816 but his position is unclear. 6. In 1798 the store was a tienda mestiza. 7. Carmón had a tienda mestiza in 1798 with a different address. 8. The name for 1807 is Don José Mariano Salas. 9. Between 1794 and 1816 there are several variations of Don José Flores' name. They may have been the same people or relatives in the same family. 10. There is a Don José Francisco Truxillo in 1807. 11. There is a Don José Miguel Carrera in 1807. 12. Muñoz owned two pulperías in 1807, and was a partner in a third. 13. This store was located at the same address in 1807, but the owner's name was Don José Fortis. It is almost certain that they are the same people or of the same family. 14. Villegas received his license in 1789, but the store's location seems different then. 15. Acevedo was in partnership in 1807 and 1816 with Don Matías Muñoz. 16. López may have been in business in 1798 also. 17. Vargas, cited as Don Francisco Xavier Vargas in 1807, owned a tienda mestiza in 1798. The tienda mestiza of 1798 (and probably 1790 also) was at the same location as the 1807 pulpería.

Table 2

MEXICO CITY GROCERS IN BUSINESS IN 1806 AND 1815*

1. Don Juan Andrade	20. Don Pedro Marcos Gutierrez
2. Don Ysidoro Broz	21. Don José Herrera
3. Don Juan Ortega	22. Don Alenogenes Justiniano
4. Don Ciriaco Cuellar	23. Don Rafael Morales
5. Don Alejandro Castillo	24. Don José Mireles
6. Don Juan Casas	25. Don Rafael Ocaña
7. Don Mariano Coronel	26. Don Emeterio Pastor
8. Don Baltasar Casanova	27. Don Ygnacio Paredes
9. Don Mariano Domínguez	28. Don Ygnacio Quijano
10. Doña Josefa Delgado	29. Don Mariano Rodríguez
11. Don Vicente Espejo	30. Don Vicente Silva
12. Don Juan Estanillo	31. Doña Teresa Torres
13. Don Domingo Gómez Sánchez	32. Don Hypolito Torices (in 1806 Don Ygnacio Torices)
14. Don Anacleto Gama	33. Don Antonio Velasco
15. Don Felix Clemente Garrido (without inventory)	34. Don Joaquín Vara
16. Don José Mariano Gallegos	35. Don Justo Vdias (now dead, daughter apparently running store)
17. Don Juan Gonzales	36. Don Domingo Ugarte
18. Don Rafael Guante	37. Don Bernardo Zuleta
19. Don Bernardo Gil	38. Don José María Zuñiga

Additionally, Don Manuel Alarcón was in business in 1811 and 1815, as were Don José Montesdeoca and Don Francisco Vanegas.

Sources:
AGNM, IG, Unidad: Real Hacienda; Fondo: Reales Cajas; Sección: Real Caja de México; "Padron general de tiendas de esta Capital formado por este Ministerio de Exercito y Real Hacienda para el arreglo del establecimiento del Derecho de Pulperias...," (compiled 1806); ibid., Serie: Pulperías, "Lista qº. Comprehende los dueños de Tiendas Pulperías en esta Corte qº. no han pagado...la Pension...," (1811); ibid., "Padron genl. de las Tiendas de esta Capital por Alfabeto de los Sugetos que las administran. Año de 1815."

functioning in 1815 (approximately 15 percent).[56] Three other stores that operated in 1815 had been open in 1811 (Table 2).[57] Ownership among these 41 stores remained constant except in two instances (Table 2). To the routine hardships confronting the grocers was now added the independence movement. It is possible that grocers were among the many Spaniards who departed Mexico during this era.[58]

The Caracas longevity figures conform to those of Puebla and Mexico City. One hundred and sixteen pulperías operated in the city during the course of 1809. Approximately 20 owners (17 percent) operated a store for at least 5 years. One hundred and nine people operated the city's 112 pulperías that functioned at some time or other during 1816. Thirty-three of them (30 percent) operated a store for at least 5 years.[59]

These business longevity figures are conservative approximations. Because partners and employees were sometimes enumerated without indication of their status or relationship to the person previously recorded in a census, it is likely that several additional grocers remained in business in each city. Nevertheless, it seems certain that for most owners the operation of a small retail grocery store was a fleeting experience.

---

[56]AGNM, IG; Unidad: Real Hacienda; Fondo: Reales Cajas; Sección: Real Caja de México, "Padron general de tiendas de esta Capital formado por este ministerio de Exercito y Real Hacienda para el arreglo del establecimiento del Derecho de Pulperias...," (compiled 1806); idem., "Padron gen¹. de las Tiendas de esta Capital por Alfabeto de los Sugetos que las administran. Año de 1815."

[57]AGNM, IG; Unidad: Real Hacienda; Fondo: Reales Cajas; Sección: Real Caja de México; Serie: Pulperías, "Lista qᵉ. Comprehende los dueños de Tiendas Pulperías en esta Corte qᵉ. no han pagado...la Pension..." (1811).

[58]Romeo Flores Caballero, *La contrarevolución en la independencia* (Mexico City, 1969), pp. 78-79.

[59]Visitas; AGNV, Real Hacienda, vol. 2423, "Año de 1816, Receptª. Admon de Alcabalas de Caracas, Quaderno de Pulperias"; ACM, *Archivos Capitulares*, vol. 2, loan contribution lists, 1821-1822. The Buenos Aires censuses used in this investigation do not lend themselves to longevity analysis. The pivotal census of 1813 (AGNA, Hacienda, X 8-4-3) does not include store addresses. However, the names of 40 of the owners of 1813 appear in the 1825 list (*Almanaque de 1826*). Approximately 453 owners operated the 502 pulperías of Buenos Aires in 1825. Discounting 5 common names, 8 percent of the grocers of 1813 displayed business longevity of at least 12 years.

NOTABLY SUCCESSFUL GROCERS

Although the majority of the small retail grocers may have endured only briefly, some not only succeeded but were quite active participants in the economy. In 1798 Don José María Campos owned both a grocery store and a tienda mestiza on the same street in Puebla. Don Domingo Larrasilla owned two tiendas mestizas and a grocery store. Don José Larrasilla owned a tienda mestiza and a grocery with "interior communication" between them.[60] In 1816 four people owned (or managed) at least two Puebla grocery stores each.[61] Apart from entrepreneurialism, one wonders how much the retail grocery operations benefited from such an intimate relationship with a potential source of supply.

As one might expect of a commercial center like Mexico City, grocers there sometimes owned at least two stores concurrently. In 1781 ten people each owned more than one retail grocery store. Seven owned two stores each; two men owned three groceries, and one man owned four of them.[62] Eleven percent of the 219 grocery stores in Mexico City were then owned by the following 5 percent of the grocers:

1. Don José Pomar   3 stores
2. Don Ignacio Izquierdo   2 stores
3. Don José de Hoyos   2 stores
4. Don Joaquín de Aldana   3 stores
5. Don Mariano Avila   2 stores
6. Don José Limón   2 stores
7. Doña María Teresa Torres   2 stores
8. Don Idelfonso Araiza   2 or 3 stores
9. Don Domingo Gil Taboada   2 stores
10. Don Manuael Larrazabal   4 stores

A similar pattern of multiple store ownership prevailed in 1806 when 9 men owned more than 1 store each. In total these 9 men owned 24 stores among them, that is, 10 percent of the city's small retail grocery

[60]AJP, FA, Roll 41 (microfilm), INAH, "Padron de Pulperías de Puebla...1798-1799."

[61]AJP, FA, Roll 41 (microfilm), INAH, "Padrón General ó reconocimiento de las Tiendas de Pulperia de esta Ciudad de Puebla..." (1816).

[62]AAM, Expediente 33, vol. 1, "Panaderías y Pulperías, 1730-1783," "Dilix*. q°. conthienen el num°. de Tiendas de Pulpería, Su Cituacion y Dueños en esta Ciudad y Sus Barrios...."

stores. Further, it is probable that another 8 men owned 20 stores.[63] Clearly some Mexico City grocers were decidedly entrepreneurial.

The Caracas grocers do not appear to have been as actively engaged in multiple store ownership as were their Mexican counterparts. For instance, in 1804 and 1807 apparently only two grocers owned more than one store simultaneously.[64] However, the purpose of the censuses of these years was supervision and not information gathering; thus it is possible that an owner was listed on one census and a partner or employee on another. Conceivably, there were several additional instances of multiple store ownership among the Caracas grocers.

Grocers in Buenos Aires also accumulated stores. In 1825, for instance, 20 men each owned at least 2 grocery stores. Together they owned 49 stores, that is, 4.4 percent of the grocers owned 9.8 percent of the city's groceries. The brothers Don Tomás and Don Nicolas Giraldes each owned 5 stores.[65]

Although the percentage of multiple store owners in the four cities was small, the actual frequency of occurrence suggests a commercial activism not consonant with the grocers' traditional reputation.

Indeed the business activities of some grocers exceeded what one would have expected of owners of small retail stores catering to the impecunious. One of the most commercially active of the grocers was Don José de Hoyos of Mexico City. When Hoyos filed a will in 1785, he owned a house in the Plazuela de Santa María de Ronda and the grocery store situated in the same building. He also owned a second grocery store in the same barrio, although the building and *aperos* (the showcases and other fixtures) belonged to other people. Additionally, he owned the inventory of a third grocery store in another part of the city.[66] When he prepared his will, Hoyos was sick and bedridden, but he survived. Two years later he was still a grocer and now also a partner in a small cloth-weaving factory. When Don Francisco de Villegas, master weaver, and his wife, Doña María Dolores Díaz, fell on bad times, Hoyos loaned the

---

[63]AGNM, IG; Unidad: Real Hacienda; Fondo: Reales Cajas; Sección: Real Caja de México," Padron general de tiendas de esta Capital formado por este Ministerio de Exercito y Real Hacienda para el arreglo del establecimiento del Derecho de Pulperias...," (compiled 1806). These are cautious estimates. It is probable that among them 15 or 17 men owned between 15 and 18 percent of the grocery stores required to pay the pulpería tax in 1806.

[64]Visitas, 1804; 1807.

[65]*Almanaque de 1826.*

[66]ANM, (Adán), vol. 1785, ff. 37-39, Will of Don José de Hoyos, 11 March 1785.

pair 500 pesos for repairs and the purchase of materials. In effect, a company was formed, with Hoyos entitled to one-half the profits. The business was placed under the management and administration of Doña María, who put up as collateral for the Hoyos "loan" a house she had inherited from her parents.[67] It is interesting that a woman played this active a role and used inherited real property to finance a business for herself and her husband.

In 1788 Hoyos filed another will. He now owned two grocery stores and lived in one of them. By this date he was owed a considerable amount of money for a small retail grocer. The estate of one person owed him 1,700 pesos; another person owed him 2,000 pesos; a third owed him 300 pesos; and a fourth person owed him 500 pesos. Some other smaller amounts were also due him. For his part Hoyos owed 1,125 pesos. Hoyos, a bachelor from Santander, Spain, named his two nephews as his heirs.[68]

The following year a new will was filed. In this document Hoyos elucidated his debt situation. One thousand pesos of the 1,700 pesos owed him by the estate of Don Domingo Conde had been advanced to Conde in the form of a loan with interest obligations--probably the standard 5 percent. No instrument was signed because the two were confident of each other and too busy to draw up the paper. Seven hundred pesos were given Conde without interest obligation, guaranteed by a personal promissory note, a *vale*. In this will Hoyos recognized part of a 4,000-peso debt he had incurred in the 1750s. It was then that he purchased a grocery store from the now deceased Don Manuel Orruño. Customarily, when a store was sold, an inventory was prepared by outside experts. However, Hoyos purchased this store without the benefit of a formal inventory. Hoyos was absent at the time and he trusted the assurances of several people he considered intelligent and conscientious concerning the value of the inventory.[69] Some 30 years later the debt had not been entirely resolved. Hoyos was a grocer whose success does not seem to have been impeded by his casual approach to business.

By 1794 Hoyos was dead, but his business ventures survived him. He willed his estate to his two nephews, the brothers Don Juan and Don Manuel Sánchez Barsenilla. When Don Juan wrote his will in 1794 he

---

[67] ANM, (Adán), vol. 1787-1789, ff. 22-23, Contract between Villegas-Díaz and Hoyos, Mexico City, 6 Feb. 1787.

[68] Ibid., ff. 69-71, Will of Don José de Ollos, 1788. His debts were his *deudas pasivas*.

[69] Ibid., Will of Don José de Hoyos, 1789. The loan to Conde was a *depósito irregular*. The loan contract not signed would have been an *escritura*. The experts who prepared official inventories were called *peritos*.

and his brother owned the two Hoyos grocery stores. As might be expected of a Hoyos heir, a good deal of money was owing and owed. There was also an additional business venture. Don Antonio García had rented a textile factory, and Don Juan introduced 1,598 pesos worth of wool, acquired either through credit or a loan. In return, Don Juan was entitled to one-half the profits. García died and was replaced in the business by his heir. Don Juan continued to fund the factory, and the financial arrangement was maintained. By 1794 he had invested, by his own count, almost 5,949 pesos in the textile operation. Of this amount, 4,500 pesos originated in the two small retail grocery stores.[70]

Another grocer who invested in an outside business was the widow Doña Juana Antonia Madueño, owner of a grocery store in the nearby villa of Coyocán. In 1789 she purchased a coach repair shop in Mexico City for 480 pesos. Half this sum belonged to her eldest son. The remaining 240 pesos belonged to her two children of minor age. The widow invested the money on her children's behalf as their tutor and as the administrator of their estate. An additional 320 pesos were contributed by the children to stock the repair shop. An administrator was brought in to run the operation for a four-year period, during which no party to the contract was permitted to withdraw for any reason. The administrator was to receive one-third of the profits until the children recovered their investment; thereafter he would be entitled to one-half the profits and be responsible for one-half the losses. Doña Juana arranged to keep close check on the administrator: he was required to record all income and expenditures, and accounts were to be settled and profits divided monthly.[71] Prior to the contract's expiration, the administrator withdrew from the relationship. Doña Juana, still the owner of a grocery store, made a verbal agreement with Don Pedro Troitiñas to operate the coach shop. In 1792 Troitiñas, a master tailor who owned a tailor shop in Mexico City, arranged to purchase the coach shop.[72]

---

[70]ANM, (Calapiz), vol. 155 (1794), ff. 391-94, Will of Don Juan Sánchez Barcenilla, 26 Sept. 1794. Like his uncle Don Juan was a bachelor from Spain. However, he fathered three children, his *hijos naturales*, whom he made his only heirs (ibid.). For an intelligent comment on the role and importance of the company in the commerce of Mexico City, see Kicza, *Colonial Entrepreneurs*, pp. 152-54.

[71]ANM, (Adán), vol. 1789, ff. 105-9, Madueño contract, Mexico City, 2 May 1789. For another mother's contribution to her child's success, see the example of Doña María Paula Velasco, daughter of a pulpero, and her son, Don José Domingo Arochi (idem., [Madariaga], vol. 1818, ff. 311-13, Velasco-Arochi contract, Mexico City, 19 Sept. 1818).

[72]ANM, (Adán), vol. 1792, ff. 141-43, Madueño-Troitiñas contract, Mexico City, 27 Sept. 1792.

Many artisans of Mexico City ventured beyond their crafts. John Kicza has observed that "master silversmiths regularly involved themselves in all sorts of undertakings in retail commerce and other fields."[73] José Manuel Infante was a silversmith who managed a grocery store.[74] In 1789 Don José Ancelmo García, master dyer, purchased a grocery store from Don Juan Gómez de Doral, who also owned a pork shop. As security, García put up the grocery store, his dye shop, and his silk shop.[75]

By the late colonial period an increasingly common form of mixed enterprise in Mexico City was the ownership of wine stores by grocers. By branching out into the wine store business the grocers could legally sell wine and spirits, just as small retail grocers normally did in many other parts of Spanish America. The wine stores of Mexico City sold local and imported wines and liquors to customers of both sexes for consumption either in or out of the store.[76] Where the customer consumed the purchase was of no small consequence to the storekeeper. The Buenos Aires grocers vigorously contested governmental efforts to terminate in-store consumption of alcoholic beverages.[77]

In branching out into wine store operations some grocers co-opted a market ordinarily withheld from them. However, there was another market also suitable for a grocery store that they did not manage to co-opt: the tens of thousands of pulque drinkers. Pulque was the easily and quickly fermented drink derived from the juice of the maguey plant. It was sold legally only in licensed *pulquerías*, 45 of which were licensed for Mexico City, most of them located away from the center of the city. Customarily imbibed in the pulquería, the beverage would have been an excellent one for the grocers to stock.[78]

[73]Kicza, *Colonial Entrepreneurs*, pp. 215-16.

[74]Ibid., p. 216.

[75]ANM, (Adán), vol. 1789, ff. 188-90, Loan contract between Don José Ancelmo García and Don Juan Gómez de Doral, Mexico City, 9 Sept. 1789.

[76]See Kicza, *Colonial Entrepreneurs*, pp. 118-21.

[77]AGNA, Interior, IX 30-4-2, Expediente 5, Leg. 26, Año de 1788, "Expediente promobido por el Gremio de los Dueños, y Administrad*. de las Pulperías de esta Capital...."

[78]Kicza, *Colonial Entrepreneurs*, pp. 121-29; and his article, "The Pulque Trade of Late Colonial Mexico City," *The Americas* 37, no. 2 (Oct. 1980): 193-221. A very low and cheap grade of pulque was sold by Indians at the central plaza (Kicza, "Pulque Trade," p. 129).

A final example of mixed enterprise is of interest. In 1795 Don Juan José Torres owned a small retail grocery store in Mexico City that he estimated to be valued at less than 1,000 pesos. He also owned two factories, one that produced noodles and another that produced starch.[79]

There were also instances of spirited commercial endeavors in Caracas and Buenos Aires, notably the activities of the previously mentioned Giraldes brothers. Between them Francisco and Tomás Giraldes owned six Buenos Aires grocery stores in 1813 with a combined value of 84,500 pesos.[80]

Not this affluent but equally active was Don Bartolomé Sotomayor. Born in the Canary Islands, he was, as the Venezuelans said, an *isleño*, as were many other Caracas storekeepers. In 1815 he was a partner in a cloth and clothing store that had a value, by his estimate, of between 13,000 and 14,000 pesos. He had contributed one-half of the principal. Just in front of this store was a pulpería that he owned outright. It had a value of 8,000 pesos, an unusually high capitalization (Table 8). Sotomayor also owned 8 houses and 13 slaves. The houses, all on a single street, were not all very valuable, 6 of them being made of adobe. Not only did Sotomayor have varied investments in Caracas, he was also involved in international trade. In conjunction with his partners from the cloth and clothing store, he had sent small quantities of indigo and cotton to Spain.[81]

---

[79]Kicza, *Colonial Entrepreneurs*, p. 113. There is a strong possibility that Don Joaquín de Aldana, who owned three pulperías in 1781 and two in 1795, owned three bakeries in 1793. In 1793 a Don José Antonio de Hoyos owned a bakery. Was he the pulpero Hoyos? Don Clemente Ortega, Don Pedro del Valle, and Don Francisco Aspiros were pulperos. There were bakers with the same names (AAM, "Abastos y Panaderías," Expediente 4, vol. 4, "Diligencias practicadas a pedimento del s.or. Procurador Síndico del Comun, en las Tiendas de Pulperia de esta Capital, sobre averiguar si venden o no el Pan comun." See also Super, "Bread and the Provisioning of Mexico City."

[80]AGNA, Hacienda, X 8-4-3, "Arreglo y Razon de...Pulperos...Agosto de 1813."

[81]RP, Escribanías, 1815 (Correa), ff. 97-100, 101-7. Part of Sotomayor's estate was 1,000 pesos that he had loaned the government for military purposes. This was a substantial amount of money; but what is more interesting than the amount is that this money belonged to the principal of the pulpería and was given to a government controlled by the royalist general Domingo de Monteverde. Monteverde was also an isleño and a royalist officer who had defeated the patriots in 1812 and brought an end to the First Republic. However, by August 1813 Simón Bolívar was back

PARTNERS

There was another kind of entrepreneur in the grocery store business, one who invested little or no capital but rather administrative effort and expertise. This was the administrating partner, a person of often very limited means who found commercial opportunity precisely because so many grocery stores were modestly capitalized. For instance, in 1805 Don José Sabino administered two Puebla grocery stores with a combined capitalization of only 1,434 pesos. A company, given a six-month longevity, had been formed with the owner of the groceries whereby Sabino invested no money but was entitled to one-third of the profits and a six-real daily allotment for food.[82] In 1800 a Caracas pulpería valued at

triumphant in Caracas. It is often said that the isleño storekeepers, of whom there were many in Caracas, were a central support of the re-established royalist government led by Monteverde. There is probably a good deal of truth to this generally accepted assertion. However, there is little evidence that the pulperos were active supporters of the Monteverde regime. This may be due to the fact that among the Caracas isleños, pulperos were not the most prominent, and their efforts on behalf of their compatriot and the royalist government may simply have gone generally unrecorded. Nevertheless, Sotomayor was one isleño pulpero who made a significant financial contribution to the royalist government. One thousand pesos was, after all, enough to capitalize a pulpería (ibid.).

[82]ANP, Notary #2, Leg. 1806, N. 719, ff. 1-30, "Autos formados á pedimento de Don Fran.co. Garcia Lobos, contra Don Josef Savino Caballero, sobre un trado de Compañía." It was not always clear who was responsible for the debt acquired by an administrator. For example, see ANP, (Mormon microfilm Roll 28,295; JIT 6049), Notary #4, 1802, ff. 12-13; ibid., 1803, ff. 28-32; and ANP, Notary #7, Leg. 1827, ff. 7-15. For the Mormon microfilm both series of numbers employed in the Mexico City reading room have been noted. An example from another business category may serve to elucidate the probable nature of partner relationships in general. In 1818 Don Bernabé Antonio de Escobedo and Don Juan Collado signed a contract to continue a company they had been operating for two additional years. Escobedo invested 53,000 pesos, and Collado some 13,082 pesos. Collado was to run the business for one-half the profits or losses. But this partner, who had put into the general fund enough money to have opened several pulperías or a good-sized tienda mestiza, was subject to stringent conditions: he was subject to Escobedo's orders and could not contravene anything the principal partner said. Collado was required to keep three books: the first was to record current accounts and the shipment of goods; the second was to note purchases and sales; and the third was to record daily expenses. Restrictions were stipulated against the purchase of illegal goods. Escobedo clearly was

753 pesos was being administered for one-third of the "profits or losses."[83] In 1838 a Caracas pulpería valued at 1,064 pesos was given over to an administrator for a half-share of the profits.[84] In the same year an unwed mother of four purchased a Caracas pulpería for 335 pesos and then turned it over to an administrator entitled to one-third of the profits.[85] In 1831 Juan de la Cruz Sefi and Manuel Marza formed a "company or mercantile Society" to establish a grocery store in San Juan. The partnership was authorized for two years with an option to renew. Sefi was required to deliver to Marza a grocery store already in operation and then valued at 408 pesos. Marza was required to administer the store and to augment its capital as much as possible. Profits and losses were to be shared equally.[86] In 1833 a San Juan grocer arranged to have his nephew administer his store, valued at 8,329 pesos, for a half-share of the profits.[87]

A clerk might become a partner. Tomás Castro administered, on a salary basis, a grocery store in Mexico City owned by Vicente Bustillo. The store was sold, and the new owner kept Castro on as an administering

---

attempting to control the operation and to protect himself from any potential wrongdoing (ANM, 1818 [Francisco de Madariaga], ff. 375-76, Escobedo-Collado contract, Mexico City, 16 Oct. 1818). According to the *Ordenanzas de Bilbao*, the colonial commercial code that governed business practice from 1737 until the new nations replaced it with their own during the nineteenth century (or as in the case of Cuba and Puerto Rico, until it was replaced by the *Código de Comercio* during the nineteenth century), all wholesale merchants were required to keep four books (Capítulo 9); as Jaime Vicens Vives phrased it: "copy books, ledgers, invoices, and copies of letters." An additional obligatory book, the journal, was added after 1783 (Jaime Vicens Vives, *An Economic History of Spain*, tr. [Princeton, 1969], p. 564). All retail stores were required by the *Ordenanzas* to keep at least one book, however informal, of all purchases and sales made on credit (Capítulo 9).

[83]RP, Escribanías, 1800 (Aramburu), ff. 59-61.

[84]RP, Protocolos, 1839 (Alvarado), ff. 11-13.

[85]Ibid., ff. 8, 18.

[86]AGPR, PN, San Juan, Caja 446, ff. 114-15.

[87]Ibid., Caja 36, ff. 732-37.

54

partner.[88] The reverse might also occur. In 1805 a Mexico City grocer sold his store but stayed on to administer it at one-half the profits.[89]

All commercial establishments potentially provided the opportunity for people to become partners in profits based on an investment of personal labor, but it was at the lower levels of the commercial scale that this opportunity was perhaps most important to society. In providing this economic opportunity the small retail grocery store may in the long run have made a contribution as significant as the provision of basic comestibles to the general population.

---

[88]Kicza, *Colonial Entrepreneurs*, pp. 113-15.

[89]Ibid.

3
Capitalization
and Profitability

CAPITALIZATION AND PAWNS

A wide range of possible capitalization, from hundreds to thousands of pesos, existed among small retail grocery stores, suggesting two interesting characteristics: first, the small retail grocery store presented the most extensive opportunity for people of limited wealth to enter a nonartisan, fixed-store commercial venture; second, there was an affluence among some grocers that would nonetheless appear unimpressive were one to peer down the socioeconomic scale from the perspective of those commercial elite, the import-export wholesale merchants.

In his 1787 petition to the town council of Puebla, the grocers' advocate Don José de Arriaga stated that most of the grocery stores "perhaps like ours, do not have a capital of thirty pesos...."[1] In 1807 the intendant of Puebla ordered a census of all small retail grocery stores in the city of Puebla to determine whether the grocer was current in pensión payments and whether the grocer possessed a valid license to operate a store. Several of the grocers reported that they had only a small amount of capital. One stated that her inventory amounted to not even 100 pesos.[2] Since the authorities were in a position to verify such statements they were probably fairly accurate. However, in 1790 a Puebla grocery store was

---

[1]AAP, Leg. 2692, Tomo 227, ff. 366-76.

[2]AJP, FA, Roll 41 (microfilm), INAH, Padrón of 1807-1808. The pensión was paid by trimester.

sold for 1,377 pesos.[3] Another was sold in 1799 for 853 pesos.[4] In 1805 a grocer owned two stores with a combined value of 1,434 pesos.[5] And in 1814 a grocery store was sold for 2,840 pesos.[6] To the extent that these valuations were representative, it was possible for people of distinctly different means to enter the grocery business.

In Mexico City also the small retail grocery store was an opportunity for people of varied means (including those with only a few hundred pesos) to invest (Table 3). However, government regulations interfered with this opportunity; during the final decades of the colonial period the "Ordenanzas para el común de los tenderos de Pulperia...,"[7] promulgated in 1757 and superseded by the "Reglamento para el gobierno y direccion de las Tiendas De Pulpería,"[8] issued in 1810, required the grocers to accept certain items of personal property as pawns (prendas) in return for comestibles. The customer was permitted to pawn items of clothing and jewelry, etc., but not religious items or household items such as plates, knives, and forks. The grocer was required to give the customer a note indicating the nature of the pawned item and the value received. Furthermore, the grocer was required to keep a record of these transactions in the form of a book. While it was not unusual for small storekeepers generally to accept items of personal property in return for goods, it was only in Mexico City and Puebla among the cities investigated that this was required by law. The authorities recognized that the grocers were in business to make a profit, so after a year (later reduced to a half-year), the pawned items could, with judicial permission, be sold.

In Puebla the grocers' advocate, Don José de Arriaga, complained about the pawning requirement in 1787.[9] Customers often did not redeem their pawns, "although three, four, six months or a year passed...." The

---

[3]ANP, Notary #5, vol. 1790-1795, f. 23.

[4]Ibid., vol. 1800.

[5]ANP, Notary #2, Leg. 1806, N. 719, ff. 1-30.

[6]ANP, Notary #7, Leg. 1814, ff. 26-27.

[7]AAM, Expediente 2, Tomo 3452; Fonseca and Urrutia, *Historia general*, 4: 332-72; Lorenzot, comp., *Ordenanzas de gremios*, pp. 167-73.

[8]BNM, Ms. Division, Ms. 1320, 20 Feb. 1810. Professor John Kicza kindly sent me a copy of the Reglamento. Both sets of regulations were signed by the viceroy but almost certainly were drafted by the town council. Although they were issued for Mexico City, they apparently affected the Puebla grocers also.

[9]AAP, Leg. 2692, Tomo 227, ff. 366-76.

Table 3

SAMPLE CAPITALIZATIONS OF GROCERY STORES AND GROCERY STORES
WITH WINE STORE OPERATIONS IN MEXICO CITY, 1775-1856

Type of Store	Date	Capitalization (rounded pesos)	Document
1. Grocer	1775	4,000 (part or all of the principal)	will
2. Grocery	1787	1,216	will
3. Grocery	1788	111	sale
4. Grocery	1788	1,083	sale
5. Grocery	1792	1,801	inventory
6. Same store	1794	1,000	sale
7. Grocery	1797	1,113	inventory
8. Grocery	1797	534	inventory
9. Grocery	1797	1,060	inventory
10. Grocery	1801	965	inventory
11. Grocery	1811	428	failure
12. Grocery-Wine store	1831	9,121	sale
13. Grocery-Wine store	1832	92	sale
14. Store ("tienda") and Wine store	1846	1,308 (approx.) the store only	inventory
15. Store ("tienda") & Wine store	1855	2,580	inventory
16. Same store	1856	1,881	sale
17. Grocery	1786	4,623	sale
18. Grocery	1787	1,894	sale
19. Grocery	1789	1,286	inventory
20. Grocery	1789	929	inventory
21. Grocery	1790	235	sale
22. Grocery	1791	4,258	sale
23. Grocery	1795	2,376	sale
24. Grocery	1795	1,360	sale
25. Grocery	1802	8,500	sale
26. Grocery	1804	1,657	sale
27. Grocery	1808	1,015	sale
28. Grocery	1813	3,900	inventory
29. Grocery	1817	1,265	inventory
30. Grocery	1825	594	inventory

Sources:
1. ANM, Morales, 1775; 2. Ibid., Adán, 1787; 3. AHH, Consulado, Leg. 482-12; 4. ANM, Adán, 1788; 5. AHH, Consulado, Leg. 492-6; 6. Ibid., Leg. 491-68; 7. AGNM, Consulados, Tomo 200, "Inbentarios formados por muerte del Sargento Don José Xaraba"; 8. Ibid.; 9. Ibid.; 10. Ibid., Tomo 164, Exped. 10; 11. AHH, Consulado, Leg. 684-12, 1811; 12. Tribunales, Papeles Sueltos, Juzgado de Letras, Año-1834; 13. Ibid.,

58

Table 4

EXAMPLES OF THE RELATIONSHIP BETWEEN INVENTORIES, APEROS, AND PAWNS*

1. The pulpería of Don Juan Monasterio, sold to Don Matías Alcedo, 1802 (AGNM, Consulados, Tomo 160).
Inventory:	4,268 pesos
Aperos:	1,200 pesos
Pawns:	3,005 pesos

2. The pulpería and vinatería of Don Nicolas Ortuño in 1855 (Tribunales, Papeles Sueltos, 1855).
Inventory:	1,861 pesos
Pawns:	210 pesos
Aperos:	Not Listed

   (The store owed 180 pesos and was owed 460 pesos.)

3. The pulpería and vinatería purchased by Don José María de los Rios in 1831 (Tribunales, Papeles Sueltos, Juzgado de Letras-Año de 1834, "Los Acreedores á la testam* del finado D. Tomas Ruiz....").
Inventory:	3,944 pesos
Aperos:	2,000 pesos
Pawns:	231 pesos

   (The store owed 497 pesos and was owed 3,443 pesos.)

4. The pulpería and vinatería of Don Fernando Dias in 1832 (Tribunales, Papeles Sueltos, 1832, "Valance de Traspaso de una Tienda....").
Inventory	87 pesos
Aperos:	100 pesos
Pawns:	51 pesos

   (The store owed 146 pesos.)

5. The pulpería of Don Francisco Ruíz Tarifa, sold in 1811 because of failure (AHH, Leg. 684-12, Consulado--Año de 1811, "Cesion de la Tienda...a favor de sus acreedores").
Inventory:	134 pesos
Aperos:	150 pesos
Pawns:	144 pesos

6. The pulpería sold by Doña María Ynes de Estrada in 1788 (AHH, Consulado, Leg. 492-12, "Balanze de Traspaso y venta Real de la Tienda de Pulpería...de la que era Dueña...D* María Ynes....").
Inventory:	40 pesos
Aperos:	50 pesos
Pawns:	21 pesos

7. The pulpería and vinatería de Don José Reymundo de Moya, sold in
1792 (AHH, Consulado, Leg. 492-6).

Inventory:	558 pesos
Aperos:	600 pesos
Pawns:	488 pesos

(The store owed 26 pesos and was owed 130 pesos.)

8. Moya received the same store back in 1794 because the financial
agreement was not fulfilled (AHH, Consulado, Leg. 491-68).

Inventory:	267 pesos
Aperos:	600 pesos
Pawns:	206 pesos

(The store owed 73 pesos.)

9. In 1797 Don José Xaraba owned three pulperías. At his death that
year, the stores were inventoried (AGNM, Consulados, Tomo 200,
"Ynbentarios formados por muerte del Sargento Don José Xaraba").

Store 1

Inventory:	467 pesos
Aperos:	500 pesos
Pawns:	166 pesos

(The store had cash on hand of 121 pesos and 12 pesos worth of
additional items not noted in the inventory, but it owed 152 pesos.)

Store 2

Inventory:	255 pesos
Aperos:	100 pesos
Pawns:	221 pesos

(This store had a few additional pesos in items and cash; it owed 53
pesos.)

Store 3

Inventory:	746 pesos
Aperos:	500 pesos
Pawns:	174 pesos

(This store had a few pesos in cash on hand and owed only 10 pesos.)

*All figures rounded.

All inventory figures in this table pertain only to items. Cash on hand and
debts owed to and by the store are not included in this category. Similar
information on five additional pulperías, taken from the consulado records
of the AGNM, is presented in Kicza, *Colonial Entrepreneurs*, pp. 117-18.

only recourse left to the grocers was to apply for a license to sell the pawns at public auction. However, during the half-year or so that the pawns were held, the grocer suffered a financial loss on the capital invested in inventory items advanced to the nonpaying customer. Not only was capital thus taken out of the business cycle, the continual nature of the pawning process rendered a part of a store's total value virtually nonliquid. In 1799 Don Pedro López petitioned the authorities in Puebla for a license to sell the pawns that had been accumulating in his grocery store since 1797. Their total value was about 104 pesos, and a list had been prepared specifying the items pawned, their value, and their owners. López was granted permission under the usual condition: an oral or written public announcement of the forthcoming auction had to be made at the store's door on each of three days. This was to provide those on the list an opportunity to redeem their pawned objects prior to the public sale, which could take place 15 days after the public announcements. Thus, the first announcement was made on July 5, the second on July 6, and the last on July 8. There were pawns of silver, rosaries, socks, shirts, and handkerchiefs, among others.[10]

Sometimes the combined value of the pawns reached disproportionately high levels. In 1805 Don José María del Valle operated a grocery store in Puebla that at the moment of failure had an inventory worth 70 pesos and pawns worth 56 pesos.[11] In this case, a reduction in the pawns perhaps would have made little difference in the store's operation. During the same year, Don José Sabino Caballero returned a grocery store he had been administering to its owner. The value of the inventory plus 18 pesos in cash was 291 pesos. The pawns totaled 156 pesos.[12]

A similar situation prevailed in Mexico City (Table 4). In 1795 Don Juan Rubín de Celís petitioned judicial officials for permission to sell the pawns held in his store more than six months. He estimated the value of the hundreds of items he had taken in at 548 pesos. The official value, established by outside assessors, was 543 pesos. There were hundreds of items of such little value that they were grouped conveniently together. Celís valued them at 253 pesos, the assessors at 254 pesos. The total official value was 797 pesos.[13] In 1811 Don Ignacio Vargas was doing so poorly in his grocery store that he was forced to cede to his creditors. In

---

[10]ANP, Notary #2, Leg. 1799.

[11]ANP, Notary #6, Leg. 1809.

[12]ANP, Notary #2, Leg. 1806, "Autos formados á pedimento de Don Fran^{co}. Garcia Lobos, contra Don Josef Savino Caballero, sobre un trato de Compañía."

[13]AHH, Consulados, Leg. 491-35.

total he owed them more than 500 pesos. His inventory was worth 134 pesos, while the pawns he had taken in were worth 144 pesos.[14] However unfortunate his circumstance, without the pawning requirement he might have had a considerably larger inventory.

Not only did the pawning requirement impinge upon the grocers' liquidity, the regulations of 1757 and 1810 required that the grocers guarantee a security of up to 500 pesos to insure the value of the pawns taken in.[15] The question arises whether someone with merely a few hundred pesos to invest could have arranged such a guarantee. Furthermore, the 1810 regulations stipulated that anyone who wanted to become a grocer must invest at least 1,000 pesos in his store. The authorities felt that those who invested less tended to tyrannize the public and commit fraud.[16] To the extent that the authorities were successful in enforcing this regulation, they would have deprived entry into the grocer ranks to many who would have had sufficient capital in other cities.

The data for Caracas and Buenos Aires are ample enough to permit an examination of grocery store capitalizations in reference to other categories of stores. In Caracas the most important merchants, the business elite, were the *comerciantes*--the import-export wholesalers. Beneath them in economic importance were the *mercaderes* (wholesalers). The merchant tribunal comprised mainly three categories of business people: *hacendados*, comerciantes, and mercaderes. It is difficult to rank store categories and storekeepers beneath this level. Generally, in declining order of capitalization, were the *tiendas de mercería*, followed by the canastillas, the bodegas, the pulperías, and finally the *ranchos*.

The tiendas de mercería were dry goods stores, basically dealing in imported goods at the retail level; they could be capitalized modestly, in the range of a bodega or a pulpería, or more highly, beyond 10,000 pesos (Tables 5-8).

Canastillas, aptly named, often tucked in corners of other stores, might sell clothing, or dry goods or hardware; their capitalizations might

[14]Ibid., Leg. 684-12.

[15]AAM, Expediente 2, Tomo 3452; Fonseca and Urrutia, *Historia general*, 4: 332-72; Lorenzot, *Ordenanzas de gremios*, pp. 167-73; BNM, Ms. 1320. In 1757 the security was made to the town council's fiel ejecutor, but in 1810 to the city's *corregidor*.

[16]BNM, Ms. 1320. There were earlier attempts to enforce a 1,000-peso minimum investment, but it is unclear how successful they were.

Table 5

CAPITALIZATION OF SOME CARACAS TIENDAS DE MERCERIA
(DRY GOODS STORES)

Name of Owner or Partners	Date	Valuation	Document
1. D. Miguel Casado de Galbán & D. José de Alsugaray	1797	5,000	Contract
2. D. Antonio Días Flores & D. Juan Dias	1797	16,751	Contract
3. D. José Hernández de Orta & D. Francisco Hernández de Orta	1797	2,234	Contract
4. D. Antonio Miguel Gonzales	1797	4,000[a]	Will
5. D. Juan José Yrastoiza & D. Juan José Lander	1798	4,000	Dissolution of Company
6. D. Juan de Yllas & D. Francisco Quintero & D. Mariano Campino	1802	14,523	Dissolution of Company
7. D. Antonio Dias Flores & D. Augustin Espino	1800	13,250	Contract
8. D. José Hernández de Orta & D. Diego Bautista Perdomo	1802	1,500	Contract
9. D. Ramón Pérez de la Portilla & D. Mateo Delgado Oramai	1802	10,771	Contract
10. Doña Juana Luisa Machado & D. José Francisco Gallegos	1803	2,640	Contract
11. D. Domingo Hernández Nuñes & D. Francisco Hernández Nuñes	1803	10,417	Contract
12. Lic. D. José Rafael Rodríguez & D. Nicolas Bello	1810	23,000 Approx.	Contract
13. D. Manuel Seballos	1813	+2,000 Perhaps	Will
14. D. Santiago Lucias	1817	7,408[a]	Will
15. D. Miguel Alcantara & D. Domingo García Espinosa	1817	23,076[b]	Contract

Notes:
[a]These two tiendas de mercería were in canastillas.
[b]This figure is for two tiendas de mercería, and they were both in canastillas.

Sources:
All of the following sources are from *Escribanías*, located in the *Registro Principal*, Caracas. 1. 1797 (Barcena), ff. 85-87; 2. 1797 (Aramburu), ff. 372-74; 3. 1797 (Aramburu), ff. 256-58; 4. 1797 (Aramburu), ff. 15-18; 5. 1798 (Aramburu), f. 1; 6. 1800 (Aramburu), ff. 2-3; 7. 1802 (Aramburu), ff. 414-16; 8. 1802 (Aramburu), ff. 15-17; 9. 1802 (Aramburu), ff. 175-76; 10. 1803 (Texera), ff. 8-10; 11. 1803 (Tirado), f. 417; 12.

Table 6

CAPITALIZATION OF SOME CARACAS CANASTILLAS

Name of Owner or Partners	Date	Valuation	Document
1. Doña María Ygnacia Bello & D. Diego Bautista Perdomo	1797	1,480	Contract
2. D. Martín Cartaya & D. José Domingo Cartaya	1802	3,809	Contract
3. D. Antonio Timudo & D. Silvestre Roxas	1805	11,000	Contract
4. D. Juan José Lander & D. Antonio Hernández de León	1813	5,208	Contract
5. D. Miguel Antonio de Oyarzabal & D. Luis Morales	1817	1,600	Contract

Sources:
All sources are from Escribanías, *Registro Principal*, Caracas. 1. 1797 (Barcena), ff. 272-73; 2. 1802 (Cobran), ff. 182-83; 3. 1805 (Ascanio), f. 90; 4. 1813 (Jimenes), ff. 47-48; 5. 1817 (Urbina), ff. 101-2.

Table 7

CAPITALIZATION OF SOME CARACAS BODEGAS
(All figures in rounded pesos)

	Name of Owner or Partners	Date	Valuation	Document
1.	D. Bartolomé García & D. Nicolás Yanes	1800	18,592	Contract
2.	D. Bartolomé de Sotomayor & D. Francisco Rodríguez Acosta	1800	10,984[a]	Contract
3.	D. Mateo Salazar & D. Vicente de León & D. José Julián Pérez	1802	9,000	Contract
4.	D. Sebastián Tovar	1802	1,350[b]	Contract
5.	D. Francisco Vaes Salazar & D. Juan Andrés Salazar	1802	6,500	Contract
6.	D. Francisco Gonzalez & D. José Ygnacio Ezguiaga	1803	9,600[c]	Contract
7.	D. Juan Maximiano Mena	1803	800	Will
8.	D. Gonzalo Padrón Castro & D. José Martínez	1803	6,373	Contract
9.	D. Nicolás Machado & D. Antonio Delgado	1803	3,463	Contract
10.	D. Vizente Oropeza & D. Francisco Gomez	1807	1,000[d]	Contract
11.	D. Santiago Parodi	1807 1809	3,125 1,125	Statement to Consulado
12.	D. Andrés Pérez & D. Domingo Pérez Sánchez	1810	5,331	Will
13.	Doña María Luisa Hidalgo & D. Luis Viera	1813	5,038	Contract
14.	Doña María Rita Miranda & D. Juan Alvarez	1814	954	Contract
15.	D. Antonio Vicente García & D. Luis García	1819	5,962	Will
16.	To D. José Pacheco	1825	2,138[e]	Contract
17.	D. Simón de Ugarte & D. Francisco Bárbara & D. José Félix	1835 or Earlier	4,000	Will

Notes:
^aThis figure is for two stores, a tienda de mercería and a bodega.
^bIn 1802 this store was a bodegón, but in 1803 it was listed a bodega.
^cThis figure is also for two stores, a tienda de mercería and a bodega.
^dThis figure may well have been a mistake in the contract. It would not be surprising if it was really 10,000 pesos.
^eThis bodega also had an almacén, that is, a warehouse.

Sources:
All Sources, except number 11, are from Escribanías, *Registro Principal*, Caracas. **1.** 1800 (Tirado or Arocha), ff. 203-4; **2.** 1800 (Aramburu), ff. 305-7; **3.** 1802 (Aramburu), ff. 486-88; **4.** 1802 (?), ff. 1-2; **5.** 1802, f. 225; **6.** 1803 (Aramburu), ff. 301-2; **7.** 1803 (Aramburu), ff. 114-18; **8.** 1803 (Cires), ff. 93-94; **9.** 1803 (Barcena), f. 89; **10.** 1807 (Santana), ff. 282-83; **11.** Mercedes M. Alvarez, *El Tribunal Del Real Consulado De Caracas*, 2 vols. (Caracas, 1967), 1: 345-59; **12.** 1810 (Ascanio), ff. 197-98; **13.** 1813 (Castillo), ff. 41-43; **14.** 1814 (Correa), ff. 26-27; **15.** 1819 (Hernández Guerra), ff. 53-56; **16.** 1825 (Barcena), f. 101; **17.** 1835, (Hernández Guerra), ff. 251-56.

Table 8

CAPITALIZATION OF SOME CARACAS PULPERIAS
(all figures in rounded pesos)

Name of Owner or Partners	Date	Valuation	Document
1. D. Juan Peres García	Prior to 1765	450	Will
2. D. Domingo Pérez Fuentes & D. Eugenio Negrón	1797	At Least 970	Will
3. D. Antonio Medina	1800	753	Will
4. D. José Francisco Trugillo	Prior to 1802	461*	Will
5. D. Juan García de la Cruz & D. Francisco Ponce	1802	984	Will
6. D. Domingo Gonzales Garrido	1802	1,700	Will
7. D. Francisco Fernandes & D. Juan José Ramires	1803	800	Contract
8. D. Pedro Gonzales Grillo & D. Miguel Alfonso	1807	1,600	Will
9. D. Juan Pérez Forte & D. Juan Padrón Sánchez	1811	2,750	Will
10. D. Bartolomé Morales & D. Juan de Castañeda Morales	1807	1,200	Will
11. D. Rafael Alvaracín	Prior to 1813	800	Will
12. D. Guillermo Morales & D. Juan Antonio Morales	1813	Approx. 1,197	Will
13. D. Bartolomé Sotomayor	1815	8,000	Will
14. D. Pedro Dias & D. Antonio Martines	1816	944	Will
15. D. Bartolomé Reyes	1820	200-300	Will
16. D. Francisco Montero	1837	1,470	Will
17. Doña Josefa Matilde Yanes	1838	335	Will
18. D. Ramón Pérez Calanche	1839	1,064	Will

*This figure might represent part of a pulpería or part payment.

Sources:
1. *Escribanías* (i.e., the notary records, become *Protocolos*, 1835, both in *Registro Principal*, Caracas), 1765 (Therreros), ff. 185-89; **2.** 1797 (Aramburu), ff. 57-62; **3.** 1800 (Aramburu), ff. 59-61; **4.** 1802 (Aramburu), ff. 494-97; **5.** 1802 (Aramburu), ff. 212-15; **6.** 1802 (Aramburu), ff. 263-64; **7.** 1803(Tirado), ff. 348-49; **8.** 1807 (Aramburu), ff. 224-26; **9.** 1807 (Hernández), ff. 131-36; **10.** 1811 (Ravelo), ff. 10-11; **11.** 1813 (Texera), ff. 86-88; **12.** 1813 (Aramburu), ff. 62-65; **13.** 1815 (Correa), ff. 97-100; **14.** 1816 (Tirado), ff. 6-8; **15.** 1820 (Texera), ff. 165-68; **16.** 1838

well be modest, comparable to that of a pulpería or a bodega (Tables 6-8).[17]

At the low end of the hierarchy were the bodegas and the pulperías, followed by ranchos, temporary street stores, and itinerant salesmen. Bodegas might be capitalized very modestly, for 1,000 or 2,000 pesos, that is, in the general range of a pulpería; or one might be capitalized between 5,000 and 10,000 pesos, or more (Table 7). Sometimes owners crossed categories, as in the case of Don Francisco González and Don José Ignacio Ezguiaga, who formed a company to operate two stores: a dry goods store and a bodega. The company was capitalized at 9,600 pesos, and both stores were located on the same corner.[18] A bodega located in the main plaza in 1800 was capitalized at 18,592 pesos.[19] At the opposite end of the continuum were two bodegas capitalized at less than 1,000 pesos, precisely within the normal range of pulpería capitalization.

Table 8 presents 18 pulpería capitalizations from a date prior to 1765 through 1839. The total number forms only a miniscule fraction of all the pulpería operations that functioned in Caracas during these decades. Nevertheless, considered with caution, the table provides an interesting array of data. Nine, certainly, and perhaps 10 of the 18 pulperías were capitalized at various moments in their histories at under 1,000 pesos. In 1803, for example, Don Francisco Fernandes and Don Juan José Ramires formed a company to operate a pulpería capitalized at 800 pesos.[20] These figures suggest that ownership of a small retail grocery store in Caracas may have been within reach of a larger percentage of the population than in Mexico City. However, to make a valid comparison it would be necessary to know more about general economic conditions in both cities, including the availability of credit. There apparently was no attempt on the part of the government to set a minimum capitalization for pulperías, as occurred in Mexico City. Nor were the Caracas grocers required to be pawnbrokers, and thus it was not

---

[17]There also existed in Caracas cloth and clothing stores not included among the canastillas, and their capitalizations were sometimes substantial. For instance, one was established in 1829 capitalized at 6,000 pesos (RP, Escribanías, 1830 [Antonio Juan Ochoa], ff. 32-33). Prior to the nineteenth century there were also "tiendas mestizas" in Caracas, but I have not seen mention of them after 1800. Probably they continued to exist under a more precise nomenclature.

[18]RP, Escribanías, 1803 (Aramburu), ff. 301-2.

[19]Ibid., 1800 (Tirado or Arocha), ff. 203-4.

[20]Ibid., 1803 (Tirado), ff. 348-49.

necessary to remove significant amounts of capital from the commercial cycle.

Grocery stores in Buenos Aires also could be capitalized very modestly. In 1813 (Table 9) more than 60 small retail grocery stores operated on investments of less than 101 pesos.[21] Furthermore, there were 235 stores capitalized at less than 501 pesos, that is 51.4 percent of the city's 457 grocery stores.

The Buenos Aires business operation most capable of supplying grocery store needs at the wholesale level was the almacén.[22] Many almacenes specialized in either alcoholic beverages, comestibles, china, or some other item or items. Some also maintained a broad retail inventory.[23] Of the 144 almacenes in Buenos Aires in 1813, the majority were capitalized in the general range of a grocery store (Table 10). Most of the almacenes were capitalized at less than 1,001 pesos, and a third

---

[21]AGNA, Hacienda, X 8-4-3, "Arreglo y Razon de la Contribucion extraordinaria que se señala a los gremios de Almaceneros, Fabricantes De Belas y Marquetas de Sebo, Jaboneros, Pulperos, y Boticarios de esta Capital...Agosto de 1813." The census of 1813 was conducted for the purpose of establishing an extraordinary tax. Presumably, the enumerators and store owners estimated store capitalizations, yet one senses a decided attempt at accuracy. Thus, while most figures are rounded in a fairly gross manner, as in 500, 200, 100, there were also such figures as 2,545, 2,919, 1,100. The storekeepers knew that the authorities could order an official inventory at any time, and, indeed, when some owners began to protest the continued tax on the grounds that their capitalization had become reduced, official inventories were taken. An example is Don José Seoane's appeal, AGNA, Hacienda (1815), X 8-4-3. For examples of differing opportunities inherent in the Buenos Aires pulpería, see idem., Appeal of Doña Ana Correa Morales, 1 Dec. 1815; Socolow, *Merchants of Buenos Aires*, pp. 78-79; AGNA, Registro de Escribano 6 (Agrelo), 1806, ff. 363-64; idem., Registro de Escribano 5 (Boyso), Años 1812-15, Will of Don Andrés Blanco, 15 July 1814; AGNA, Tribunales, Comerciales, Letra M, Años 1831-33, Leg. 184 "Don Joaquín Rute en representacion de Don Salvador Moreno contra Con Ciriaco Oliver, sobre disolución de una Compañía."

[22]See the brief definition in *Almanaque de 1826*, p. 155.

[23]An example of a contract for the formation of an almacén is in AGNA, Registro de Escribano 4 (Iranzuaga), 1815, ff. 128v-130. A financial breakdown of an almacén, including inventory items, is to be found in idem., Tribunales, Comerciales, Leg. 181, Letra M, Años 1825-1828. Some stores, simply referred to as "tiendas," sold a broad range of goods at both wholesale and retail, except for alcoholic beverages and comestibles (*Almanaque de 1826*, p. 203).

Table 9

CAPITALIZATION OF BUENOS AIRES GROCERY STORES IN 1813*

Pulpería Capitalization (in pesos)	Relative Frequency (as a percent)	Number of Pulperías (N = 457)
0-50	3.7	17
51-100	9.8	45
101-500	37.9	173
501-1,000	14.4	66
1,001-2,000	13.3	61
2,001-3,000	4.8	22
3,001-4,000	3.7	17
4,001-5,000	1.5	7
5,001-10,000	6.6	30
10,001-15,000	.07	3
15,001-20,000	1.1	5
20,001-30,000	.04	2
30,000+	2.0	9

*The percentages in this and the following table do not reach 100 because the numbers are rounded.
*Source: AGNA, Hacienda, X 8-4-3, "Arreglo y Razon de la Contribucion extraordinaria que se señala a los gremios de Almaceneros, Fabricantes De Belas y Marquetas de Sebo, Jaboneros, Pulperos y Boticarios de esta Capital...Agosto de 1813."

Table 10

CAPITALIZATION OF BUENOS AIRES ALMACENES IN 1813*

Almacén Capitalization (in pesos)	Relative Frequency (as a percent)	Number of Almacenes (N = 144)
0-50	0	0
51-100	2.1	3
101-500	34.0	49
501-1,000	20.1	29
1,001-2,000	26.4	38
2,001-3,000	6.3	9
3,001-4,000	5.6	8
4,001-5,000	.69	1
5,001-10,000	4.2	6
10,000+	.69	1

*Source: AGNA, Hacienda, X 8-4-3, "Arreglo y Razon de la Contribucion extraordinaria que se señala a los gremios de Almaceneros, Fabricantes De Belas y Marquetas de Sebo, Jaboneros, Pulperos y Boticarios de esta Capital...Agosto de 1813."

were capitalized at less than 501 pesos,[24] demonstrating that in Buenos Aires many small retail grocers had the financial capacity to become wholesalers.

PROFITS

The central issue was, of course, profits, yet the grocers rarely alluded to them. Profitability may be calculated in either of two ways: on the basis of sales; or on the basis of capital investment. The French agent Depons stated that the owners of the Caracas bodegas and pulperías sold no article for less than 100 percent profit and often two and three times that amount.[25] This is anecdotal and probably a gross exaggeration. Town councils in Caracas and elsewhere set maximum prices on many of the items sold in the small retail grocery stores, and it is unlikely that they would have permitted such a high rate of profit on necessities. For instance, the Mexican regulations of 1757 permitted the grocers a profit of one real on every peso's worth of bread acquired from the bakers, that is, a profit of 12.5 percent. However, whether the profit on sales was 12.5 or 100 percent, what was important to the storekeeper was how rapidly the inventory was sold. Thus, if a Mexico City grocer obtained 16 loaves of bread for a peso on the basis of two or three days of credit, sold the entire lot in a day or so, received another 16 loaves, and maintained this cycle, considerable profits would have accrued both on sales and investment.

Ultimately, however, the critical rate of profitability was the one based on capital investment. The administrator of a small store (of unspecified nature) in the town of Izúcar in the intendancy of Puebla

---

[24]AGNA, Hacienda, X 8-4-3, "Arreglo y Razon de la Contribucion extraordinaria...de Pulperos...Agosto de 1813." There are many examples of credit obligations to almaceneros totaling 1,000 or more pesos. In 1778, for instance, Don Jaime Frasqueri purchased goods from the almacén of Don Bernardo Gregorio de las Heras for the sum of 2,249 pesos (AGNA, Registro de Escribano 6 [Echaburu], 1788, ff. 272-73). During the 1820s an almacenero sold goods valued at 4,386 pesos to the owner of a pulpería in Quilmes (idem., Tribunales, Comerciales, Leg. 184, Letra M, Años 1831-1833, Don Manual Murrieta contra Don Rumaldo Caneva). Usually, generous terms were offered to large-scale purchasers, such as a half-year at no interest. After that time the purchaser was required to pay .5 percent interest per month on the outstanding debt. One example is the Jausoro obligation to Lizaur, AGNA, Registro de Escribano 4 (Iranzuaga), 1815, ff. 25v-26.

[25]Depons, *Travels in South America*, 2: 74.

stated that during four months in 1814 a 100-peso principal had "yielded free of all my expenses 25 pesos."[26] If this were repeated periodically the store was truly a profit maker. However, information from other categories of stores suggests that such a rate of profitability on investment was not commonplace. In 1809, for instance, Don Joseph María Ramírez lost the Puebla bakery that he had established with 3,496 pesos provided by an investor entitled to one-half the profits. Ramírez claimed that the business had never produced more than 500 pesos of profit a year.[27] This was about 14 percent, and it had to be divided in half.

Nor did grocery stores routinely earn very high rates of return. Don Manuel Alvarez de Palacios administered a grocery store and a wine store in Mexico City in 1800-1801 with a combined principal of 1,494 pesos. According to Alvarez, during a 17-month period the two stores generated a profit of 334 pesos, less 58 pesos borrowed for stock purchases. This represents a profit of 276 pesos, or 18.5 percent.[28] However, the owner received only half of this amount over the 17 months.

In November 1854 Don Nicolas Ortuño established a combined grocery and wine store in Mexico City capitalized at 2,289 pesos. In January 1856 he sold the business to Doña Tomasa Ruíz. As of early December 1855, the business had yielded a profit of 292 pesos, of which the owner was entitled to half, approximately 6 percent.[29]

One grocer provided detailed information regarding profitability. In 1829 Don Manuel Sánchez owned a combined grocery and wine store in Mexico City that was closed down by a town councilman, *Regidor* Don Manuel Sabas Avila, for alleged police violations. Sánchez immediately appealed to one of the city's alcaldes to have the store reopened, and the appeal was granted. Furthermore, the grocer demanded lost revenue from the town councilman.[30] For the two days that his store had been kept

---

[26]AJP, FA, Roll 40 (microfilm), INAH, legajo--Año--Izúcar.

[27]ANP, Notary #6, Leg. 1809, Ramírez petition. See also the Puebla tienda mestiza owned by Don José María Lamegos. The store may have produced a profit of about 5 percent over three and one-half months, but Lamegos was entitled to only half (idem., Notary #2, Leg. 1816, "Balance finalizado en 29 Agosto del año de 1816...Dn. José María Lamegos...").

[28]AGNM, Consulado, Tomo 164, Expediente 10, Alvarez vs. Torres.

[29]Tribunales, Papeles Sueltos, 3 Dec. 1855, "Balance pª reconocer el estado que guarda la casa de comercio...pertenece al Sr. D. Nicolas Ortuño...."

[30]Ibid., Año de 1829, Sánchez vs. Sabas Avila. The significant documentation runs some 50 folios. One of the advantages of a combined grocery-wine store was that the wine stores were required to be closed at

closed, Sánchez estimated a loss of 50 pesos in gross revenue daily.[31] He also believed that the attention being paid to the case had reduced his revenue. Consequently, he presented the authorities a chart of revenues for the days 13 May through 21 May 1829. For each day he indicated his revenue and the difference between that figure and 50 pesos, the sum he

---

times when grocery stores were required to be open, meaning that in combination alcoholic beverages were sometimes sold when a wine store would have been closed. However, a ruling of 1824, repeated in 1829, stated that combined stores that sold "licores" were subject to the same laws and penalties pertaining to wine stores (as the regidor observed in ibid.). Sabas Avila might well have known the regulations concerning *vinaterías* since he owned one himself, and, what is more, it was located at the same corner as Sánchez's (Mariano Galván Rivera, comp., *Guía de forasteros de México para el año de 1829* [Mexico, 1829], p. 74). Although the position of the regidor on the town council of Mexico City still conveyed social prestige and political influence, it was not as important a post as it had been during the colonial period, and men with less than great wealth could secure it. This change in the nature of the town council was called to my attention by Linda Arnold.

[31]Tribunales, Papeles Sueltos, Año de 1829, Sánchez vs. Sabas Avila. To this figure Sánchez added additional legal costs, bringing the total to 98 pesos 1/8 real. It was this final amount that Sánchez demanded of Regidor Sabas Avila. On 14 December 1829 Alcalde Don Antonio Barreda ruled that the regidor must place 98 pesos in the hands of the authorities until final exceptions were made by the regidor. Sabas Avila replied that he did not have enough cash to fulfill the obligation, this from a member of the town council of Mexico City Initial official entreaties failed to secure the 98 pesos. On 15 December Sabas Avila and a government official agreed on the substitution of some *alhajas* for the 98 pesos. On 19 December Alcalde Barreda ruled that the regidor must pay the 98 pesos, and he embargoed the alhajas. The litigation continued into 1830; still Sánchez was unable to collect his 98 pesos. In February Sabas Avila wrote a strong complaint against the whole affair. On 27 February, an alcalde ruled against Sabas Avila and ordered the embargoed alhajas sold. In March troubles arose over the valuation of the alhajas. Now Regidor Sabas Avila appealed to the district governor. The alcalde responded that jurisdiction belonged to the city. What began as a small storekeeping issue, an alleged infraction of a relatively minor police regulation, developed into a major confrontation between a storekeeper and a town councilman, between that councilman and the town council, and ultimately between the town council and a superior administrative agency. At mid-April the matter was still in litigation, and Sánchez had not received his 98 pesos (ibid.).

obviously considered his average daily revenue. Following is a chart based on Sánchez's own records.[32]

Day	Revenue	Short
13	21.3 rr	23.44 rr
14	34.2	15.6
15	29.2	20.6
16	31.5	18.3
17	28.4	21.4
18	25.32	24.42
19	29.32	20.42
20	36.14	13.64
21	34.04	15.74

274 ps. 6 1/2 rr.

For the nine days, Sánchez stated that he had lost 274 pesos, 6 1/2 reales worth of gross revenue. Further, he stated that on the basis of a profit of 1 1/2 reales on each peso of income he had lost 51.4 1/8 pesos in profits.[33] Sánchez did not provide the kind of information necessary for an estimation of his profit on investment, but it is instructive to learn that he would use 1 1/2 reales as a standard of profit per peso of gross income. He certainly knew that the authorities were capable of confirming this figure with other grocers, which means that he could confidently state in an official document that he generally earned a profit of 18.75 percent on sales revenue in his combined grocery-wine store.

It is unfortunate that Sánchez did not indicate his store's capitalization. Since the wine store operation was closed some days and hours when the grocery store was open, Sánchez may not have averaged 50 pesos in gross sales every day of the year; thus, the 18.75 percent figure suggests handsome profits on capitalization. If the combined store were capitalized at 5,000 pesos, there would have been a profit of more than 50 percent on investment. If the store were capitalized as high as 10,000 pesos, the profit on capital investment still would have been greater than Sánchez could have hoped for on a secured commercial investment through the loaning out of money.[34]

---

[32]Ibid.

[33]Ibid.

[34]The grocery store owned by Don Tomás Ruiz in 1831 was valued at 9,121 pesos (ibid., Juzgado de Letras, Año-1834, "Los acreedores á la testam". del finado D. Tomás Ruiz..."). Naturally, such a store might be capitalized for significantly less. See, for example, ibid., 8 May 1846, "D.

74

The Sánchez profit figure is even more impressive in view of the pawning requirement, which removed capital from the commercial cycle. Furthermore, Mexican grocers often invested more money in the fixtures of the trade, such as showcases, than grocers of the other cities investigated, further limiting the potential for inventory expansion.[35]

Manuel Martinez Solicitando esperas de sus acredores..."; and ibid., 3 Dec. 1855, "Balance...pertenece al Sr. D. Nicolas Ortuño...."

[35]See Table 4.

4
Problems of
Grocery Store Ownership

Problems confronting the grocers were those intrinsic to the store's internal operation, such as credit and inventory acquisition, and those occasioned by external influences, primarily governmental interference. Some internal problems were mundane. In 1787 the Puebla grocers complained to the authorities that because "our trade is by nature excessively dirty, our clothing or uniform deteriorates much more than other people's; for its neatness and cleanliness additional costs are incurred."[1] When underscoring the "leanness" of their capital in 1813, the Puebla grocers remarked that their inventories were being consumed by rats.[2]

Other problems were complex and not readily solved. Mexican grocers were particularly troubled by their employees and administrators.[3] In Puebla at least one servant-porter (*mozo*) had to be employed to enable

---

[1]AAP, Leg. 2692, Tomo 227, ff. 366-76.

[2]AAP, Leg. 2387, Tomo 204, ff. 299-331.

[3]In order of descending importance, the following employment hierarchy prevailed in Puebla: administrator; chief clerk (*cajero mayor*); clerk (*cajero*), *dependiente*; porter or general servant. A chief clerk-administrator combination was possible. Interventors were appointed to run a store during a legal suit or bankruptcy proceedings. In Puebla a *depositario* served basically the same role as the interventor. "*Encargado*" and "*Por Encargado de*" are terms indicating temporary administrative responsibility, including representation of a store's owner at official inquiries. The terms employed in Puebla had somewhat different usage in Mexico City, where for instance, dependiente was used to describe any store employee. In Puebla dependientes were clerks with less administrative responsibility than the cajeros.

the grocer to leave the store "in search of daily inventory purchases."[4] The salary and maintenance for such employees ascended to 16 pesos monthly, which is "the least we can give them, being men of worth and value." However, in addition, these employees pilfered.[5] The owner of a Puebla grocery store informed an intendant's inquiry of 1807-1808 that he did not have a license because the person he had placed in charge of the store fled, carrying with him "papers, books and more...."[6] The administrator of another grocery store told the same inquiry that his predecessor had fled because of a discovery that had been made in the store.[7] Perhaps illegal goods had been found, or perhaps in an inner patio he was operating a prostitution scheme, as female grocers in Santiago, Chile were accused of doing at the end of the colonial period.[8]

Administrators sometimes acquired debt that the owners considered unauthorized, as occurred when Don Manuel Alvarez de Palacios expanded the inventory for a grocery store and a wine store in Mexico City owned by the *Licenciado* Don José María de Torres y Cataño.[9] Don Ramón Garrido administered a grocery store in Mexico City that suffered from a limited inventory. Like Alvarez, Garrido expanded the store's debt, precipitating a long and complex litigation with the deceased's family.[10]

Naturally, not all relationships between employees and owners ended in unpleasant litigation. Ranging through a broad spectrum of notary records, John Kicza deduced that in the whole of commerce, clerks

---

[4] AAP, Leg. 2692, Tomo 227, ff. 366-76.

[5] Ibid.

[6] AJP, FA, Roll 41 (microfilm), INAH, Padrón of 1807-1808. Owners fled also. Don Santos Gonzales was the owner of pulpería number 45, corner of Cruz de Piedra. Because the owner fled in debt, the store was being operated by an interventor until its sale could be arranged (ibid.).

[7] Ibid.

[8] Medina, ed., *Cosas de la colonia*, p. 89.

[9] AGNM, Consulado, Expediente 10, Tomo 164, "Don Manuel Alvarez de Palacios con El Lic^do. D. José María de Torres y Cataño...." On employer-employee problems, see Kicza, *Colonial Entrepreneurs*.

[10] AGNM, Consulado, vol. 51, "Cessión de una tienda de Pulpería...hecha por D. Ramón Garrido...."

"typically named their employers as executors and often as heirs."[11] In 1787 Don José de Hoyo's clerk named him his heir.[12]

The Puebla grocers were troubled especially by two problems not originating in the store itself. The first was the previously mentioned pawning requirement, set in place by the viceroy in 1757 for Mexico City but apparently applicable in Puebla also.[13] Likewise of great concern to

---

[11]Kicza, *Colonial Entrepreneurs*, pp. 136-37.

[12]ANM, (Adán), 1787, ff. 236-50; 1789, ff. 121-24. In his study of business and society in Mexico City during the late colonial period, John Kicza has described clerks of the larger commercial firms. Generally, he observes, the clerks (including chief clerks) did not earn "enough to provide more than a subsistence living" (Kicza, *Colonial Entrepreneurs*, pp. 137-38). In 1816 officials of the treasury carried out a census of all "Comerciantes" in the eight major barrios of Mexico City (AHH, Consulados, Leg. 426-16, "Padrón General de los Comerciantes que abriga esta Capital en sus Ocho Quarteles mayores...."). The annual salaries of all employees are given. However, the nomenclature in the census is used very carelessly. Except in rare instances, when the term "pulpería" is employed the general term "tienda" is used to include pulpería. Unfortunately it also includes tiendas mestizas. Further, the census of 1816 does not list such stores as chocolate stores, confectionary stores, or bakeries. Notwithstanding, approximately 30 of the tiendas of 1816 can be identified as having been pulperías in 1816 or shortly before or after that date. Approximately 20 employee salaries have been identified, ranging from 72 to 200 pesos per annum. Seven salaries were 100 pesos; 5 were 150 pesos; and 3 were 200 pesos. There was one 300-peso salary, but the store may not have been a pulpería. From the perspective of the large commercial establishments these salaries suggest subsistence, but from the perspective of the lower levels of the economy they suggest a modicum of success. For a general view of commercial establishments in Mexico City in 1816, see Jorge González Angulo, "Establecimientos comerciales, 1816," in *Investigaciones sobre la historia de la ciudad de Mexico, 1*, coordinator, Alejandra Moreno Toscano (Mexico City, 1974), pp. 105-16.

[13]AAM, Expediente 2, Tomo 3452; Fonseca and Urrutia, *Historia general*, 4: 332-72; Lorenzot, comp., *Ordenanzas de gremios*, pp. 167-73. The 1757 regulations also stipulated that each grocery store must maintain a lighted lamppost until 10 p.m. every night, and then again during emergencies. Arriaga stated that the grocers' employees wanted additional salary for caring for the lights, and although it was certain that the presence of lights was of much public benefit, "it cannot be denied that it is with great prejudice...and damage to us" (AAP, Leg. 2692, Tomo 227, ff. 366-76).

78

the Puebla grocers were the limitations stipulated in the 1757 regulations (and repeated in 1810) on plaza purchases such as chickens, eggs, birds, fruit, cheese, greens, and firewood, typically brought to town by Indians. However, a group of itinerant street merchants, called regatones, commonly intercepted the Indians before they arrived in Puebla, purchased their stock, and then sold it to the grocers. In 1787 the grocers complained that these hucksters "give us what their whim classifies as good or bad; necessary or not necessary; desirable or worthless...."[14] After "throwing into the street the bad and rotten, not only can we not make profits, but not even costs, rather only losses."[15] In 1801 the Puebla grocers appealed to the town council to prevent interception of plaza items. Further, the grocers wanted to be able to make purchases in the plazas at all hours of the day. For decades they had not been permitted to make plaza purchases prior to 10 a.m.[16] This regulation was designed to allow enterprising citizens the opportunity of buying provisions before purchases by the grocers caused shortages. However, the grocers maintained that by the time they were permitted to purchase goods in the plaza they often could not find what they wanted, nor at reasonable prices.[17] Since the regatones were an extralegal and untaxed group who disrupted the basic system for provisioning the city, the town council partially supported the grocers. Regulations against the regatones were reiterated in 1802 and ordered enforced.[18] However, the town council continued to restrict the grocers from the plaza prior to 10 a.m.[19]

Not surprisingly, the operation of small retail grocery stores was complicated by the independence movement. Greater financial contribution was required from the Puebla grocers than ever before, and just when they were earning less due to reduced traffic from outside the

---

[14]AAP, Leg. 2692, Tomo 227, ff. 366-76.

[15]Ibid.

[16]AAM, Expediente 2, Tomo 3452; Fonseca and Urrutia, *Historia general*, 4: 332-72; Lorenzot, comp., *Ordenanzas de gremios*, pp. 167-73; the regulation was repeated in 1810 (BNM, Ms. Division, Ms. 1320, 20 Feb. 1810).

[17]AAP, Expediente 943, Tomo 85, ff. 303-26.

[18]Ibid.

[19]Ibid. The ruling concerning the 10 a.m. hour for plaza purchases was sent to higher authorities for approval.

city.[20]   Additionally, the grocers were receiving copper money in payment, while their suppliers were refusing to accept copper, insisting on payment in silver.[21]

Of the grocers investigated, only those of Mexico City were officially organized by government regulation. The "Ordenanzas para el común de los tenderos de Pulperia..." of 1757 continued the organization of small retail grocers previously established, now requiring the grocers to meet together in the offices of the town council for the purpose of electing six deputies from among themselves.[22] The six oldest grocers in the city were to be appointed additional deputies.[23] The grocers were also required to elect an *"apoderado general"* for a three-year term. The apoderado represented the grocers before the authorities, handled all litigation on their behalf, supervised their activities, and enforced

[20]AAP, Leg. 2387, Tomo 204, ff. 299-331. Generally speaking, the early nineteenth century brought with it problems for storekeepers. In 1807 Don Andrés Moro had to cede his store, perhaps a tienda mestiza, to his creditors. In petitioning the city for permission to do so, he referred to the "notorious contretemps" and the commercial inertia in Puebla (ANP, Notary #6, Leg. 1806, Moro papers, 22 ff.). Don Juan Manuel De Corres had a store in Izúcar that was ruined when the insurgents entered the province of Puebla. Subsequently he opened a grocery in Mexico City, but he soon failed (Tribunales, Papeles Sueltos, "Don Juan Manuel De Corres, Dueño en propiedad...." and "Balance formal...").

[21]AAP, Leg. 2387, Tomo 204, ff. 299-331. To my knowledge there is no comprehensive study of the money situation during the late colonial and early national periods. An interesting table that compares the currencies of Spanish America and other parts of the world in 1854 is in the *Boletín histórico de Puerto Rico* 13: 317-19.

[22]AAM, Expediente 2, Tomo 3452; Fonseca and Urrutia, *Historia general*, 4: 332-72; Lorenzot, comp., *Ordenanzas de gremios*, pp. 167-73.

[23]Previously the grocers had six deputies in total (ibid.). The election of 1786 is in AAM, Tomo 3453, "Panaderias y Pulperias, 1784 a 1872," Tomo 2. The town council ordered all owners of small retail grocery stores to meet at the council's Sala Capitular on 1 December 1786 at 3:30 p.m. for the election. Not all owners appeared and apparently some of those present were administrators rather than owners (ibid).

regulations.[24] For instance, the apoderado was required to collect the levy that all grocers paid in lieu of the sales tax.[25]

The government agency charged with supervision of the grocers was the town council through the offices of its Fiel Ejecutoria. Each grocer was required to register with the Fiel Ejecutoria within 15 days of the publication of the Ordinances.[26] The fiel ejecutor determined the amount of security, up to 500 pesos, each grocer was required to guarantee to insure the value of the pawns that might be taken in.[27]

Many of the regulations of 1757 burdened the grocers; the most consequential became the pawning requirement. The regulations against establishing stores at mid-block limited the grocers' geographical options; the prohibition against intercepting goods before they reached town markets limited the grocers' acquisition of inventory. A further encumbrance was the limit on profit permitted on the sale of bread.[28]

Other regulations were also onerous. In recognition of the fundamental role of the small retail grocery store, grocers were not permitted to use the half *tlaco*; rather, they could use only coin that divided the half tlaco into four parts. Thus the monetary unit of daily trade would be a fraction of a real, geared to the needs of the poorer residents so dependent upon the grocery stores for their daily provisions. Beyond that, a new grocery store owner was required to recognize all tlacos issued by his predecessor. Consequently, the new owner had to

---

[24]AAM, Expediente 2, Tomo 3452; Fonseca and Urrutia, *Historia general*, 4: 332-72; Lorenzot, comp., *Ordenanzas de gremios*, pp. 167-73.

[25]The apoderado was required to collect eight reales per month for groceries of first class; six for second class; and four for third class (ibid.). This is the only mention that I have seen for such a class categorization and differential in the pensión system of Mexico City.

[26]Ibid. Prospective grocers were required to register with the town council and there secure a license to operate. Those desiring to sell their stores were required to inform the municipality in order to facilitate the transfer of licenses (ibid.).

[27]Ibid.

[28]Ibid. Furthermore, the grocers were not permitted to become bakers, tallow-chandlers, or pork butchers, even in partnership, although they were permitted to sell items produced by these trades (ibid.).

accept coin issued by a previous owner without guarantee that it could be used for his own purchases.[29]

All grocery stores were required to close at 10 p.m.[30] The superseding regulations of 1810 stipulated that all such stores must remain open from either 5:30 or 6:00 in the morning until 10:00 in the evening.[31]

Each grocer was required to provide a lamppost in front of his store, the light to burn until 10 p.m. However, in the event of an emergency, such as "a fire," the grocer was required to light the lamp regardless of hour. All grocers within five blocks of the emergency were also required to light their lamps.[32] This requirement meant that either the grocer's family, a family member, or an employee would have had to sleep in the store. Conceivably, some grocers who lived a considerable distance from their stores were compelled to employ someone not otherwise needed. But the imposition went further: the Ordinances noted that some city corners, including important ones, were without small retail grocery stores. The grocers as a group were therefore required to establish and maintain lampposts and lamps at those corners at their joint expense.[33] Thus the authorities enjoyed advantage in having the grocers legally organized.

Regulations also governed personal conduct. The grocers were not permitted to "ensnare" customers from the street, nor "provoke" or say "dishonest words" to the women who came to the store to make their purchases.[34] Penalties were severe: for the first offense 100 lashes; for the second 100 lashes and two years' confinement in a penal labor camp. However, these penalties were aimed directly at people "of color," since those offenders not "of color" were to suffer a fine of 10 pesos and a month in jail for the first offense and 20 pesos and two years in exile for

---

[29]Ibid. For an informative study of Mexican money, see Miguel L. Muñoz, *Tlacos y pilones: la moneda del pueblo de México* (Mexico City, 1976).

[30]AAM, Expediente 2, Tomo 3452; Fonseca and Urrutia, *Historia general*, 4: 332-72; Lorenzot, comp., *Ordenanzas de gremios*, pp. 167-73.

[31]BNM, Ms. Division, Ms. 1320, 20 Feb. 1810. No mention was made of Sundays.

[32]AAM, Expediente 2, Tomo 3452; Fonseca & Urrutia, *Historia general*, 4: 332-72; Lorenzot, comp., *Ordenanzas de gremios*, pp. 167-73.

[33]Ibid. The regulation referred only to those stores at corners. Those stores then located at mid-block were required to terminate operations (ibid.).

[34]Ibid.

82

the second infraction.[35]   Although less harsh, these latter penalties nevertheless left the regulation's intention intact.

It is clear from the regulations of 1757 that the grocers functioned in a market economy in which governmental intrusion limited their range of activity and personal choice in crucial business matters. Furthermore, not everyone was permitted to become a grocer; the regulations stipulated that no "Negro, Mulatto," or other person of color was permitted to be a grocer or administer a grocery store. All whites, Indians, people of mixed white-Indian blood, and women were permitted to own or administer grocery stores; the ability to read, write, and count was of no matter.[36]

With only a minor adjustment, the regulations of 1757 governed the activities of the Mexico City grocers until the issuance of the "Reglamento para el Gobierno y Dirección de las Tiendas de Pulpería," in 1810.[37] This ordinance differed only slightly from its predecessor,[38] with one significant distinction: not content with regulating the small

---

[35]Ibid.

[36]Ibid. Two other regulations are of interest. In accordance with the Laws of the Indies, grocers who were in the military, or "*del Santo Oficio*," were denied trial by special courts (*Recopilación*, 1: 125, 561-62). Thus the grocers could be prosecuted by the civil authorities for infractions of the regulations. Another article prohibited the grocers from attracting to their own stores a servant-porter (mozo) employed by another grocer, and no servant-porter was permitted to leave his employment in one grocery store for work in another unless the second store was situated at least 400 varas (nearly 400 yards) from the first. At the bottom of the grocery store's employee hierarchy, the servant-porters were evidently important enough to a store's operation to warrant such a limitation on both them and their employers.

[37]BNM, Ms. Division, Ms. 1320, 20 Feb. 1810.

[38]The ordinance of 1810 presented a succinct definition of pulperías: these were the stores that sold comestibles and other items at retail, such as candles, charcoal, lard, chile, and beans. These stores were different from the tiendas mestizas, which sold comestibles, grain, and other items by the pound and larger units. The pulperías functioned on the basis of tlacos and took in pawns. If the tiendas mestizas received pawns, they were required to matriculate among the pulperías. The new regulations permitted pulperías to be established not only at street corners but wherever the grocer desired. A form of competition was permitted, with women and poor people allowed to sell firewood, charcoal, brown bread, lime, fruit, and green vegetables, but not any other items stocked by the pulperías. The women and poor people were permitted to sell from *accesorías* (ibid.).

storekeepers for tax collection purposes, the authorities now attempted to control the quality of trade itself. Not only were prospective owners required to matriculate among the other grocers and obtain a license, they had to be "fit for and intelligent in the trade." Furthermore, the prospective grocers were required to invest at least 1,000 pesos in their stores. Responsibility for evaluating each situation and informing the authorities concerning the desirability of granting a license was given to the grocer deputies and the apoderado.[39]

The degree to which the Mexico City grocers were supervised is illustrated by their problems over bread. In 1793 the viceroy of Mexico ruled that all bakers and storekeepers must sell to the public both common and superior bread.[40] The purpose of the ruling was to insure that the common bread was sold throughout the city, making it available to the great masses of poorer residents. In response to the viceregal ruling, the town council assigned every grocery store in the city to a particular bakery and stipulated that the grocers could purchase their bread solely from that bakery. The grocers, through their apoderado, Don José Xaraba, vigorously protested the new market arrangements. Xaraba argued that it would be less offensive to allocate the number of customers for the storekeepers than to mandate the baker-grocer relationship. Above all, the arrangement was "contrary to freedom of trade...."[41]

---

[39]Ibid.

[40]AAM, "Abastos y Panaderías, Expediente 4, vol. 4, "Diligencias practicadas a pedimento del S.º. Procurador Síndico del Comun, en las Tiendas de Pulperia de esta Capital, sobre averiguar si venden o no el Pan comun." See also Aida Castilleja, "Asignación del espacio urbano: el gremio de los panaderos, 1770-1793," in Ciudad de Mexico: ensayo de construcción de una historia, coordinator, Alejandra Moreno Toscano (Mexico City, 1978), pp. 37-47. By storekeepers the viceroy meant pulperías or other very small stores that traded in pulpería items. In fact, these latter stores were probably legally pulperías. The common bread was pan común and the superior bread was pan floreado. At the moment, a loaf of superior bread was required to be 21 ounces, while a loaf of common bread was one-third larger (ibid.). See also John C. Super, "Bread and the Provisioning of Mexico City."

[41]AAM, "Abastos y Panaderías, Expediente 4, vol. 4, "Diligencias...en las Tiendas de Pulperia...si venden o no el Pan comun." Xaraba took the position that the Fiel Ejecutoria of the town council lacked the authority to interfere in the affairs of those pulperías that were not of the category of ordenanza, which were approximately 20 of the 157 recorded pulperías of 1793. Although simply dismissed by the authorities, this was a rather bold position for the grocers to assume, suggesting the confidence that could be

In 1793 every grocer and baker in Mexico City was informed of the new regulations. Two years later a survey of each grocery store was taken to determine whether common bread was being sold as required.[42] Remarkably, not one of the 157 grocery stores visited by the authorities sold common bread. One store indicated that it sold no bread of any kind. Almost all the others stated that they did not sell common bread; some administrators said that they did not know why they did not sell it. Most owners who were present during the official visit stated that they did not sell the common bread because their customers refused to purchase it or did not like it. Some owners said they simply could not acquire this kind of bread.[43] Although it is unclear what remedial action was taken, it is interesting that the city's small retail grocers would simply thwart rulings by both the viceregal and municipal governments, rendering government control more illusory than the regulations might suggest.

The Mexican grocers were also subject to the limited jurisdiction of the merchant tribunal, which as a court heard bankruptcy cases. Creditors appealed to the merchant tribunal to have a store sold and debts paid. Storekeepers appealed to the tribunal to carry out the sale of a store's inventory in order to pay off creditors. Financial conflicts between the storekeeper and a creditor might be adjudicated by the merchant tribunal.[44] Conflicts between the storekeeper and a customer would not likely reach the tribunal since problems involving modest sums of money were traditionally resolved by minor judges at the barrio level or by alcaldes. These conflicts were usually adjudicated verbally (the *juicios verbales*), depriving posterity of a potentially rich source of information about the daily lives of the grocers.

One of the most perplexing problems confronting the Mexican grocers concerned the militia. For more than two centuries the Spanish government chose to keep its colonial populations as unarmed and untrained militarily as it deemed possible. However, the British occupation of Havana and Manila in 1762 altered these circumstances, inspiring a new defense policy that raised regular infantry and dragoon regiments in the colonies, rotated Spanish units, and placed Spanish and

---

mustered when small retail grocers were gathered together in a formal organization and provided with a spokesman.

[42]Ibid.

[43]Ibid.

[44]Or the seller of a grocery store might appeal to the tribunal to force payment from the purchaser or the guarantor, as in the case of Don Juan Monasterio's litigation against the guarantor Don Bartolo Alcedo (AGNM, Consulados, Tomo 160, Monasterio-Alcedo papers). See also the interesting case involving a provincial grocery store in 1809 in ibid., vol. 75, Valdés vs. Padre Francisco de la Concha, Año de 1809.

other European officers and soldiers in the colonies on permanent assignment.[45] Because of the empire's size and the Crown's limited finances, the essence of any new defense policy inevitably had to be a colonial militia.

For small retail storekeepers and other merchants, membership in the militia units conveyed advantages. The uniform and a seeming parity with officers and soldiers born in Spain were a source of pride.[46] The privilege of military jurisdiction in criminal and civil cases was sometimes employed by royal officials as a recruitment tool. In many instances it was successful: Archer has noted that this privilege "remained one of the best means of attracting candidates even after it became quite evident that a militia commission was not always advantageous to the holder."[47]

Yet there were serious disadvantages in belonging to the militia. Militiamen sometimes could be transferred to regular army units.[48] Furthermore, militia service meant time away from home and business. For a grocer this meant time away from the store on days when the store would ordinarily be open. In 1794 the merchant tribunal appealed to the viceroy to reduce the burden of militia service that had been placed on the commercial community. Arguing the case for the grocers, the tribunal

[45]Archer, *Army in Bourbon Mexico,* pp. 9-10. A royal decree of 1793 placed all soldiers under military jurisdiction in both civil and criminal matters, thus depriving both the town council and the merchant tribunal of jurisdiction over retailers who were in the militia. Within days after the publication of the royal order one official claimed that the illegal drink *chinguirito* (a low-grade rum) had appeared in at least three wine stores whose owners were members of the Urban Regiment and who claimed military jurisdiction for themselves (ibid., p. 181). Christon Archer has provided an example of a grocer's involvement in a jurisdictional dispute. A grocer name Yriarte had ordered some meat supplies from a pork butcher for his grocery store. Yriarte did not pay and the pork butcher appealed to the barrio alcalde, who already had a complaint from a merchant who had supplied the grocer with sugar and grain. The alcalde went to the grocery store where he encountered a group of 28 people there to reclaim pawns. It turned out that the grocer had sold the pawns without legal permission. When asked with what authorization he had sold them, Yriarte replied that he had needed none. The merchant tribunal concluded from the grocer's attitude that he intended to invoke military jurisdiction; thus in May 1794 it had him forcibly removed from the militia barracks and placed in the public jail (ibid., p. 182).

[46]Ibid., p. 210.

[47]Ibid., p. 152; see also pp. 126-27.

[48]Ibid., p. 152.

noted that monthly militia assemblies took place on festival days, forcing owners of grocery and other stores whose servants were in the militia to close on such days.[49] Further, the tribunal observed, many of these were marginal operations to begin with.[50] In 1801 a group of merchants presented a petition in which they claimed that since the mobilization of the Urban Regiment of Commerce in 1794, more than 150 shops had closed in Mexico City.[51]

It was difficult for grocers to escape service in Mexico City's Urban Regiment of Commerce. Sanctioned by the Crown in 1693, it had been established the previous year in an effort to control rioting in the city. Until the 1760s the Urban Regiment was a rather rag-tag battalion that required little service of its members, but then the situation altered. When regular units had to be transferred out of the capital, the Urban Regiment of Commerce was required to provide greater service, even being mobilized for years at a time, with some members of the regiment serving on active duty many days annually. While affluent members were able to send clerks or hire replacements,[52] the less affluent had to serve or send an employee who might have been needed to make plaza purchases or to remain in the store while the owner made trips to the plaza.

Grocers were numerous in the Urban Regiment of Commerce. In 1808, for instance, Barrio Number Four had 334 residents who were members of the regiment. However, only 168 of them were physically able for active service. Fifty-three of the total number were grocers, but only three of them were unable to serve, and this was due to age. Thus there was in this instance a disproportionate number of small retail grocers among members of the Urban Regiment.[53] This may have resulted from patriotic zeal or the more practical impulse to protect their property. Certainly their militia numbers reflected also their high visibility as fixed storekeepers and their inability to escape service.[54]

Excessive enterprise brought the Caracas grocers into conflict with the local authorities. Toward the end of the eighteenth century, grocers

---

[49]Ibid.; AGNM, IGG, vol. 60-B, Consulado to Viceroy Branciforte, 8 Aug. 1794.

[50]Ibid.

[51]Archer, *Army in Bourbon Mexico*, p. 188; AGNM, IGG, vol. 42-A.

[52]Archer, *Army in Bourbon Mexico*, pp. 168, 178.

[53]AHH, Consulado, Expediente 2, Leg. 663, "Padron del Quartel N°.4...."

[54]Many young men did escape the military census enumerators (Archer, *Army in Bourbon Mexico*, p. 152).

controlled much of the city's firewood trade, and in 1786 they were prohibited from traveling out of the city for the purpose of purchasing wood for resale.[55] In 1787 there was a bread scandal in the city, and the municipal government publicly censured the grocers for selling impure bread.[56] Later in the century several grocers smuggled corn into the city at night for sale at high prices to city bakers, just at a time when the municipal government was attempting to regulate the supply of flour.[57]

One of the most intractable problems confronting small retail grocers in Venezuela, Mexico, and probably many other Spanish American colonies, was the general shortage of small currency. Where there existed no small currency, as in Medellín, New Granada, until the reforms of the 1780s, there were no pulperías.[58] The grocers of Caracas resorted to issuing their own personal currency, commonly referred to as *señas*. These were issued by the individual storekeeper in denominations of one-half, or one-quarter of a silver real. Two serious problems attended the issuance of señas. First, they were personal issues, unbacked, and one grocer was not obliged to accept señas issued by another grocer. Second, the grocer who accepted the coin of another grocer who subsequently went bankrupt prior to redemption faced a potential loss. The issue was complex, and the government did not resolve it in the best way possible-- through the issuance of appropriately small currency in sufficient quantity. Instead, it elected to control the symptoms rather than the causes of the problem. In 1783 the town council mandated that each grocer must register with the town council a mark for the señas he or she might issue. Thus the municipal government was institutionalizing a previously informal minting system. In an attempt to protect those customers and grocers who held señas from a store that closed, the town council required that each grocer have a guarantor for all señas issued, the guarantee to be

---

[55]AGNV, Capitanía General, Diversos, vol. 60, ff. 237-50, "Bando de buen Govo de este año de 86." The prohibiting edict stipulated that no one might legally purchase wood for the purpose of reselling it until 24 hours had passed since its arrival in the city (ibid.). The restriction was repeated in 1811 (*Actas del cabildo de Caracas, 1810-1811*, vol. 1 [Caracas, 1971], pp. 84-86, 138).

[56]Waldron, "Social History," p. 276.

[57]Ibid.

[58]Ann Twinam, "Miners, Merchants, and Farmers: The Roots of Entrepreneurship in Antioquia, 1763-1810" (Ph.D. diss., Yale University, 1976), pp. 103, 106.

in ordinary currency.[59]   Notwithstanding these reforms, problems with currency continued to trouble the grocers and their customers. In 1801 some grocers complained to the municipal government that many people refused to accept their señas. By this time there were so many señas in circulation (some counterfeit), that it was not always possible to determine a coin's worth.[60]

The Caracas authorities, like their Mexico City counterparts, attempted to protect customers from personal abuse. Many of the grocers and employees were men and bachelors, while many of the customers were women and unmarried. In both the pulperías and bodegas there were instances of personal misconduct.[61]   In response the municipal government ruled during the early 1770s that no single women could enter a pulpería or bodega but rather had to make purchases through the store's windows.[62] The governor of Caracas ruled that no bachelor or married man whose wife was not resident in Caracas could operate a pulpería or a bodega, but the Crown reversed this ruling and permitted bachelors and married men whose wives were absent (doubtless directed at the many isleños with wives resident in the Canary Islands) to operate these stores.[63]

---

[59]ACM, Actas del Cabildo, 5 Aug. 1783, f. 94; Waldron, "Social History," p. 277.

[60]Waldron, "Social History," p. 277.

[61]The issue of moral rectitude may have been compounded by the fact that many of the pulperos and bodegueros (and their employees) were isleños, men who seem generally to have maintained themselves aloof from creole society. At times the isleños may have comprised a majority of the pulperos, but this is difficult to determine precisely. During the eighteenth century a city ordinance required that every store in Caracas be inhabited day and night. The isleños seem to have preferred to entrust their stores at night to relatives (ibid., pp. 11-12).

[62]Ibid., p. 278. A suggested public edict of 1770 placed restrictions on the selling of arms to blacks or castes by the grocers (ACM, Actas del Cabildo, 1770-1771, Jan. 1770, f. 1).

[63]AGNV, La Colonia, Intendencia de Ejercito y Real Hacienda, Real Cédulas, Real Cédula de 20 Jan. 1777. This is a 62-page typescript of the 180-page manuscript original. On page 27 of the typescript (p. 104 of the manuscript) the statement reads: "...de hoy en adelante no solamente los casados sino tambien los solteros pueden tener pulperías." The date of the governor's ruling is unclear. The Crown's reversal occurred in January 1777. Because the merchant tribunal was uninterested in the pulperías a potentially important source of data was never realized. However, the

The Buenos Aires grocers were also subject to several jurisdictions. As elsewhere, the immediate supervisory agency was the town council. Beyond normal business matters the town council had a special interest in the grocery stores: these paid a tax called *composición*; 30 of the stores paid the tax to the town council, while the rest paid it to the royal treasury.[64] Most grocery stores came under the jurisdiction of the merchant tribunal under whose purview fell all store owners with investments of at least 150 pesos.[65] The viceroy and intendant also concerned themselves directly in the lives of the grocers, just as they sometimes did in other colonies.

At approximately the same time that the Crown created the merchant tribunal in 1794 it also created the merchant militia units.

---

tribunal did maintain jurisdiction over the bodegas. One bodega case is especially interesting. Don Santiago Parodi owned a bodega administered by Don Rafael Suarez. During a litigation between the two, Suarez stated that when he took charge of the Parodi bodega for one-third of profits and losses he had already been running it for five or six months on a salaried basis, and he did not know the store's value when the arrangement changed. Furthermore, he stated that he did not know how to read or write (Alvarez, *Tribunal del real consulado de Caracas*, 1: 345-59). One would think that an administrator would have known a store's value before beginning to run it for a share in profits. It is noteworthy also that an illiterate could administer a bodega.

[64]Examples of composición tax collections are in AGNA, Pulperías, IX 13-8-13, "Libro que formamos los Ministros Generales de Real Hacienda De esta Capital...del Real Derecho de Composición del Pulpero"; "Quaderno de Composicion de Pulperias...del presente año de 1806"; "Razon de las Pulperías qᵉ Tiene a Su Cargo el mui Ylustre Cavildo [1808]." Examples of Receipts for composición tax payments are in ibid., Division Gobierno, Sección Gobierno, Padrones, derechos, etc. 1795-1811. On the early history of the composición tax see Bossio, *Historia de las pulperías*, pp. 136-39. The pulperos also paid an alcabala tax. As in many other places it was really a fee rather than a tax derived from each retail sale. Receipts for alcabala tax payments are in AGNA, Pulperías, IX 13-8-13. Additionally, the pulperos paid a tax on alcoholic beverages, the *compostura* tax. The records of the town council are replete with examples of efforts to control the pulperías. In 1786 the council urged the intendant to increase the number of pulperías to 100 (surely those of composición) (*Acuerdos del extinguido cabildo de Buenos Aires* (Buenos Aires, 1930), Serie 3, Tomo 8, p. 210).

[65]Germán O.E. Tjarks, *El consulado de Buenos Aires y sus proyecciones en la historia*, 2 vols. (Buenos Aires, 1962?), 1: 54-55. For many years the merchant tribunal collected the sales tax (Ibid., 2: 479-84).

Although Buenos Aires was vulnerable to foreign attack, most large wholesale merchants sought to minimize their militia obligations. Small retail storekeepers were required to serve, and many of them also resented the burden.[66]

While many problems confronted the Buenos Aires grocers, one central, overriding issue troubled them: the grocers and the town council maintained divergent views concerning the basic nature of a small retail grocery store. The town council wanted the grocery stores to be nothing more nor less than basic food suppliers. The grocers, for their part, wanted customers to spend time in their stores chatting and otherwise socializing, that is, consuming alcoholic beverages. That was the crux of the matter; the Buenos Aires grocery stores were to varying degrees drinking houses. However, with drinking went excesses that were universal enough: drunkenness, foul language, brawls, deaths. The city fathers desired to stop this, but in their attempts to do so they came up against a group of grocers able to thwart them through legal action.

In 1788 the town council issued rules governing the operation of the Buenos Aires grocery stores. A group of grocers joined together and shortly challenged two articles.[67] The grocers authorized Don Juan de Almeria, an attorney attached to the royal government, to represent them. The two articles in question, numbers three and five, stipulated that in order to avoid "excesses," counters must be placed at the door of each

[66]Ibid., 1: 198-201; Socolow, *Merchants of Buenos Aires*, pp. 114-20. Socolow has noted a merchant appeal for relief from militia service that was supported by "wholesalers, retailers, food suppliers and clerks" (p. 114).

[67]AGNA, Interior, IX 30-4-2, Expediente 5, Leg. 26, Año de 1788, "Expediente promobido por el Gremio de los Dueños, y Administrad". de las Pulperías de esta Capital...." In 1775 an interim governor issued several rules governing the activities of the pulperos (Facultad de Filosofía, Universidad de Buenos Aires, *Documentos para la historia del virreinato del Río de la Plata*, 3 vols. [Buenos Aires, 1912-13], 1: 25-29). In 1790 the viceroy issued rules governing the operation of the pulperías. Among other things the pulperos were ordered not to permit vagrants into their stores. They were not to sell comestibles and other items at immoderate prices. And pulperías were to close at 10 p.m. in winter and at 11 p.m. in summer (AGNA, Pulperías, IX 13-8-13). Much of the material covered in the remainder of this chapter is treated well in Bossio, *Historia de las pulperías*, pp. 26-46. There is interesting material in his book on the pre-1750 period, especially pp. 107-9, 219-27. There are also worthwhile references to rural pulperías, pp. 49-63, 240-47. On rural pulperías see Richard Slatta, "Pulperías and Contraband Capitalism in Nineteenth-Century Buenos Aires Province," *The Americas* 38, no. 3 (Jan. 1982): 347-62.

grocery store with no interior access permitted to customers. From these counters would be dispatched "the drinks and other items of provision...."[68] This regulation would have altered the fundamental nature of the city's grocery stores. The town fathers drew upon the example of Seville for their position. The grocers' advocate responded that Buenos Aires was not Seville, where streets were paved. In Buenos Aires, he asserted, the streets were founts of thick dust carried by the continuous winds, the worse during the rainy season. Additionally, in Seville, Almeria pointed out, customers travelled on foot and thus fraud was not easily committed. On the contrary, in Buenos Aires customers generally went about on horseback, with the new regulation they would be able to ask for what they needed while mounted. To prevent a customer's fast getaway without paying, a grocer might feel obliged to request payment in advance, suggesting a lack of confidence in his clientele.[69] The articles in question were suspended on an interim basis while the authorities considered the matter.[70]

In an attempt to bypass the town council the grocers petitioned the intendant for a ruling in their favor.[71] Relying on information presented by the city's chief attorney, the intendant observed that in the city's grocery stores there were daily scuffles among the customers, resulting in wounds and deaths. Furthermore, slaves left the service of their masters for the entertainment offered by the grocery stores: drinking, guitar playing, and card games. The attorney did not want any customers to enter the stores, and the intendant supported his position, ruling that within 20 days of the publication of his decree, counters must be placed as stipulated in the new regulations and no customer of either sex might enter

---

[68] AGNA, Interior, IX 30-4-2, Expediente 5, Leg. 26 Año de 1788, "Expediente...de los Dueños...de las Pulperías de esta Capital...."

[69] Ibid. Considering that it was 1778, Almeria presented a sophisticated argument in stating that laws and statutes should accommodate circumstances, place, and time, and vary accordingly. A law that is useful and convenient in one province might be prejudicial in another. Furthermore, he pointed out, other cities in Spain were not subject to the same regulations as those of Seville, and therefore he questioned, why should Buenos Aires be subject to such regulations? What is more, the Buenos Aires pulperos, unlike their counterparts in Spain, were contributing two taxes to the royal treasury (probably, the compostura tax on alcoholic beverage and the composición tax), and they rendered great service in the militia regiments, attending themselves or sending paid replacements (ibid.).

[70] Ibid.

[71] Ibid.

the stores. All drinks and food supplies had to be sold in a vessel for home consumption.[72]

Clearly, this portended a radical change in the basic function of the grocery stores. The city's attorney had stated his position unequivocally: he wanted the grocery store to be a provisioning rather than a gambling house. With the intendant's decision announced, the grocers appealed to the royal audiencia.[73]

At this juncture an interesting turn of events transpired. In an attempt to render the regulations unnecessary, the grocers suggested that six or more deputies be selected to supervise the city's grocers and stop any bad business practices. In response, the royal audiencia ordered the city's attorney to pick eight grocers to supervise the construction of the counters that were ordered placed at the grocery doors. Evidently, nine deputies were elected by the owners and administrators of the city's grocery stores. In 1789 the deputies proposed that a guild of grocers be formed under specific rules. Since the guild would supervise the practices of all grocers, they suggested, the offensive regulations would no longer be needed.[74] In Mexico the government brought the grocers together in an organization, but in Buenos Aires the grocers themselves sponsored such an arrangement. The deputies went on to suggest exactly what the town council of Mexico City later proposed: the elimination of the very small grocery stores. The Buenos Aires grocers suggested that each grocery store should have a capitalization of at least 500 pesos. Any less, they urged, led to adulterated drinks, "gatherings of vicious people," and games, among other things. Further, the deputies wanted to close all grocery stores currently capitalized at less than 500 pesos. They thought that licenses should be granted only to proper people. Most grocers, administrators and employees were "españoles," by which the deputies meant "white." Castes and Negroes might undermine order, apart from the fact that few of them could put together a well-stocked store, and thus should be admitted to the trade only with reasonable cause and careful inspection of their conduct, collateral, and financial ability to supply a proper store.[75] If grocery store capitalizations in 1789 were somewhat

---

[72]The ruling is also in ibid. In his reply the intendant presented a concise definition of small retail grocery stores: they were stores that sold "at retail every kind of comestibles and drinks most used by the common people" (ibid.).

[73]Ibid.

[74]Ibid.

[75]Ibid.

similar to those of 1813, perhaps between one-third and one-half of the city's grocery stores would have been forced to close.[76]

The legal battle over the placement of counters continued into the nineteenth century. In 1812 the intendant of police ordered the grocers to place their counters at the doors to impede traffic into the stores. The grocers replied to the order with the old arguments, to which the intendant of police responded that the public would be better served if the counters were placed at the store doors.[77] The issue was then taken up by a court of appeals, which with slight modification ruled in favor of the intendant's proposals, a decision later supported by the national government.[78] What occurred following this setback is unclear; however, Buenos Aires grocery stores evidently continued to function as drinking houses.[79]

The Buenos Aires grocers, as did their colleagues in Mexico and Caracas, had a problem over bread. During the final decades of the colonial period the town council issued an arancel on bread which permitted bakers to earn two pesos on each fanega (about 1 1/2 bushels) of wheat fabricated into bread. Since the arancel fixed the retail price of bread, the profit was assured by permitting the weight of a 1/2-real loaf of bread to vary according to the price of wheat.[80] To save employee costs and to assure themselves that the grocers would purchase all the bread they produced, the bakers began to withdraw from the retail end of the business. As further inducement, the bakers sold to the grocers at a discount of one real on each peso's worth of bread, which meant a reduction in the bakers' profits.[81]

In 1782 the bakers initiated a campaign to have the arancel altered or terminated. The bakers argued that in the present circumstances they were not able to make a profit on bread. The fiel ejecutor of the town council, Don Antonio Obligado, answered that if this were so, the problem

[76]The inflationary pressures during the independence period would not likely have produced 1813 capitalizations generally less than those of 1789.

[77]AGNA, Interior, IX 30-4-2, Expediente 5, Leg. 26, Año de 1788, "Expediente...de los Dueños...de las Pulperías de esta Capital...."

[78]Ibid.

[79]This seems certain from the nature of store inventories (Chapter 1, notes 20, 23-25).

[80]Lyman L. Johnson, "The Artisans of Buenos Aires During the Viceroyalty, 1776-1810" (Ph.D. diss., The University of Connecticut, 1974), p. 208.

[81]Ibid, p. 210.

was not the arancel but rather the practice of giving over to the grocers the retail end of the business. Obligado judged that the issue was that the bakers had become so dependent on the grocers that the latter were able to force up the discount from 1/2 real to 1 1/2 reales. This is where the problem for the grocers arose. Obligado felt that the grocers were making too much profit merely selling bread to the public, concluding that the town council either would have to end the wholesale discount to the grocers or prohibit the sale of bread in their stores. A litigation ensued during which Obligado requested that the intendant issue an edict ending the sale of bread in grocery stores.[82]

The problem over bread was intertwined with the confrontation over the basic nature of a grocery store. Obligado wanted to prohibit the grocers from selling bread, arguing that many artisans and journeymen, sure that the grocers would sell them bread on credit, did not trouble to work. They abandoned their tasks as well as their families. Although Obligado found an evil in this, it should be noted that the extension of credit for the purchase of bread was one of the grocer's most important social services. However, Obligado knew that men entered the grocery stores to purchase bread on credit, but knowing that it was this item that the grocers least preferred to sell on credit, they would request one-half or one real's worth of aguardiente, an item the grocers sold on credit for greater gain. One thing would lead to another, others would join them, more drinks of aguardiente would be consumed, and the men would leave the stores drunk. Obligado's argument parallels the case made for the placement of counters at the grocery store doors. He was concerned about fights and afflictions to wives and families. And, he pressed, it would be a great service if there were fewer grocery stores.[83]

One additional point made by Obligado is of consequence. The fiel ejecutor noted that the grocers routinely gave change in the form of goods rather than coin, and the most common item used for this purpose was a glass of aguardiente. It is not surprising that grocers would "make change" with an inventory item that could be measured at minute levels. However, to the degree that they were making change with aguardiente, the grocers were courting official disapproval at the wrong time. Obligado feared that women and children who entered the grocery store solely for bread received aguardiente also.[84] This additional challenge to the traditional nature of the grocery stores of Buenos Aires failed, and the

---

[82]Ibid., pp. 210-15.

[83]*Documentos para la historia del Virreinato*, 2: 61-62; Johnson, "Artisans of Buenos Aires," p. 216.

[84]This point of Obligado's was not published in the document but apparently was in the original record (Personal communication from Professor Johnson, 10 December 1981).

relationship between the city's bakers and grocers continued through the colonial period.[85]

Of special interest is a further problem that confronted the grocers, this one caused by their sale of shoes. During the 1790s the shoemakers of Buenos Aires attempted unsuccessfully to form an official guild.[86] The ordinances proposed for the shoemakers' guild sought to stop the sale of locally produced shoes in any shops other than those of master shoemakers. This restriction was aimed mainly at the sale of cheap, ready-made domestic shoes in the city's grocery stores. The ordinances however stipulated that eight or more grocery stores or shops in various parts of the city would be permitted as legal outlets for all types of shoes. Soon the shoemakers petitioned the viceroy to publish the restrictions against the sale of locally produced shoes in grocery stores, requesting that the grocers be given two months in which to sell any shoes they held in stock. After the two-month period, the shoemakers wanted all remaining shoes confiscated and fines imposed. The viceroy approved the petition and published the restrictions. Although an attempt was made by the shoemakers to lessen the impact of the restrictions, over 200 pairs of shoes were soon seized; however fines were not levied.[87]

This dispute over the sale of locally produced ready-made shoes in grocery stores resulted in a confrontation between the grocers and the shoemakers. At first the grocers acquiesced in the shoemakers' right to prohibit such trade, while trying to salvage something out of their predicament. They argued that two months was too short a time for the liquidation of their inventories, and they wanted compensation for confiscated goods.[88] Arguments from both sides ensued. The grocers, through their legal representative, Don José Moreno y Calderón, made two telling points. One was a reiteration of the universal service rendered by small retail grocery stores: they provided cheap goods to the public on credit. The grocers observed that they had "sold these shoes to the public, especially the poor, as a well-recognized benefit, since we did not require full and immediate payment."[89] The second point was that since the king refused to approve the guild's ordinances, the restrictions were not legal. The shoemakers continued to argue their own position, but by the end of 1794 representatives of the shoemakers and grocers worked out a

---

[85]Johnson, "Artisans of Buenos Aires," p. 217.

[86]Ibid., abstract, n.p. No artisan group was able to form a guild or a sodality during the colonial period (ibid.).

[87]Ibid., pp. 128-33.

[88]Ibid., p. 133.

[89]Quoted in ibid., p. 134.

96

compensation arrangement for those shoes that had been confiscated, and that ended the matter for a while.[90]

But the shoemakers continued their efforts to form a guild. Ordinances for racially separated guilds were presented to the town council for approval at the end of the decade. However, in 1799 the attorney for the town council argued against the formation of the guilds, asserting that the shoemakers, by attempting to deny the grocers the right to sell ready-made shoes, were depriving the public of cheap footwear. The attorney, as Lyman L. Johnson has observed, was making a case against monopoly.[91] Accordingly, the town council refused to approve racially separated guilds, and by 1800 the shoemakers gave up their campaign to found a guild.[92]

Significantly, not only did many of the city's grocers sell shoes, some actually underwrote and controlled what Johnson has referred to as a "nascent 'putting out' system...."[93] The grocers supplied some of the shoemakers with raw materials and arranged to purchase the finished product at a predetermined price.[94] These small storekeepers were acting as preindustrial manufacturers.

---

[90]Ibid., p. 134.

[91]Ibid., pp. 135-37.

[92]Ibid., pp. 138, 143.

[93]Ibid., abstract, n.p.

[94]Personal communication from Professor Johnson, 24 September 1981. There may be some universality of the phenomenon of preindustrial small storekeepers arranging and financing a putting-out shoemaking system. See the example of Lynn, Massachusetts, in the early nineteenth century described by Alan Dawley, *Class and Community: The Industrial Revolution in Lynn* (Cambridge, pb.,1976), pp. 25-29.

5
Conclusion

This book has been about small-scale, that is, petty capitalism.[1] It has been about entrepreneurship, about people participating in the market economy by investing their own or borrowed money to become proprietors of fixed stores. It has been about extraordinary successes and many failures. As a case study it is a contradiction of the so-called "dependency" theory. The grocers flourished or failed without regard to international capitalism, except insofar as wars, famines, excesses in production, etc., randomly affected the general population.

By way of summary, it is worthwhile to pose several generalizations that may be drawn from the foregoing data.

---

[1]Capitalism here means simply that the restrictive colonial and then national economies were to varying degrees based upon money, exchange, private property, and the profit motive. For one sensible historian's confrontation with the term "capitalism," see Braudel, *Wheels of Commerce*, pp. 231-32. See also Braudel's typically encompassing account of the development of shops and shopkeeping (pp. 60-75). Braudel considered the early shopkeeper "a capitalist in a very small way" (p. 73). And indeed the retail grocers of Spanish America were capitalists in a small way. The terms "petty" and "small" manifestly describe the scale rather than the substance of their businesses. For an interesting discussion of terminology of capitalist enterprise at the beginning of the economic continuum, see Sol Tax, *Penny Capitalism: A Guatemalan Indian Economy*, 2nd ed. (New York, 1972), pp. 13-14. In studying the "perfectly competitive" "money economy" of a Guatemalan Indian village organized around "single households," Tax desired a term for the economic unit that went beyond satisfaction of consumption needs, that is, sought profit. Thus he settled on "penny capitalism" to indicate an "intermediate class" situated between household and firm (p. 13 n.10).

THE MARKET ECONOMY

The grocers functioned in a market economy, that is, they purchased goods to sell to other people. But the market in which they participated was only partially free, both in the colonial and national periods. Many artificial restraints were set against the grocers. Town councils routinely established maximum prices on certain items and, as in the case of bread, maximum profits; and they sometimes determined days and hours of operation. In Venezuela the pulperos were not permitted to sell imported items, and in Mexico they could not sell alcoholic beverages, unless they added a wine store operation. In Buenos Aires the shoemakers attempted to deprive the grocers of the right to sell ready-made shoes. Further, town councils sponsored public markets, and these sold competing items. Nor were the grocers permitted to go out into the countryside to acquire items for resale in their stores. Rather, local governments took pains to insure that these items arrived for initial sale in the public markets.

Other restrictions were burdensome. The Mexican requirement that the grocers take in pawns in exchange for comestibles was an intrusion into the free market process, one that sometimes prejudiced a store's viability. The requirement to guarantee (through a bondsman) up to a 500-peso security for pawned items must have eliminated many otherwise eligible poor people from entering the grocer ranks. The early nineteenth-century legal minimum of a 1,000-peso capital investment for Mexican grocery stores must have done likewise. But grocers themselves attempted to deprive the less affluent from continuing in or entering the trade, as happened in Buenos Aires. The colonial Mexican government prohibited free people of color from becoming fixed storekeepers, a blatant undermining of one of the benefits of a free market economy.

Yet, if people had the cash or credit and a good deal of initiative, they could open a store or two or three of them. Beyond certain inventory restrictions, which applied to the competition also, they could stock what they chose, in whatever combination and quantity. They could sell their stores, buy others, move on.

CREDIT

The small retail grocers functioned largely on the basis of credit. They purchased many inventory items, and sometimes their stores also, on credit, and they routinely sold to their customers on credit. As the Buenos Aires grocers intimated, selling cheap items to the poor on the basis of credit was one of their most important social contributions. And it was credit that rendered the small retail grocery store an entry-level business opportunity for many people who would have been closed out of fixed entrepreneurial ventures were credit not so easily obtainable.

THE FEMALE GROCERS

The data presented in this book support the current perception of women as active participants in the colonial and early nineteenth-century economy despite restrictions in law and custom. Women were partners, owners of multiple-businesses, and inheritors who were patently aggressive in their investments. Some women demonstrated a keen awareness of legal niceties and protected their own acquisitions even within a marriage. However, women were not represented in great numbers among the retail grocers in the cities studied in this book. They were not only a small minority but in the one city where reliable data exist covering the entire grocer population, Buenos Aires in 1813, not a single grocery store valued at more than 3,000 pesos was apparently owned by a woman.

THE GROCERS AS A CLASS

In his excellent study of the town council of Puebla, Reinhard Liehr concluded that a middle class had not become established in the city by the early nineteenth century, or if so, only to a minor degree. From the point of view of division of income, the municipal population was divided basically into two classes, a "small upper class and a great lower class."[2] In a gross sense this is correct. Liehr quotes Bishop Manuel Abad y Queipo: "there are not gradations or intermediary classes, only poor and rich, plebians and nobles."[3] Nevertheless, many of the grocers were not in a meaningful sense part of the "great lower class," nor were they "plebians." But did the small retail grocers form an incipient middle class? There is no indication that the grocers formed a social class at all.[4]

---

[2] Liehr, *Ayuntamiento y oligarquía en Puebla*, 1: 55.

[3] Ibid.

[4] E.J. Hobsbawm's comment on "class" is worth repeating: "Class in the full sense only comes into existence at the historical moment when classes begin to acquire consciousness of themselves as such." This is from his

Too great a range of success and failure existed among them for a social consciousness to have developed based on mutual status and interests. This is perhaps best exemplified by the attempt of the affluent Buenos Aires grocers to eliminate from the trade the less successful. Setting aside the contentious term "middle class," it may be generalized that most of the small retail grocers in the cities investigated were situated socially and economically above the great mass of poor and below the elite. They were part of a broad middle group, not yet possessed of a unique consciousness.

THE GROCERS IN INTERNATIONAL PERSPECTIVE

It is worthwhile to consider the grocers in relation to their counterparts outside of Spanish America. For this purpose the great port metropolis of New York City, then still only Manhattan, was selected. New York was a city of spirited political factions and easy franchise requirements. The various political parties courted the artisans, the grocers, and other middling and petty storekeepers. Practically all grocers, even the very modest, could vote for a variety of public offices.[5]

"Class Consciousness in History," in *Aspects of History and Class Consciousness*, ed. István Mészaros (New York, 1972), pp. 5-21.

[5]During the late eighteenth and early nineteenth centuries, all adult free men who satisfied a minimal residency requirement and possessed a freehold worth $50, or paid an annual rent of at least $5 could vote for state assemblymen and federal congressmen. This encompassed the majority of the adult free male population and excluded only the poorest and transients (Howard B. Rock, *Artisans of the New Republic: The Tradesmen of New York City in the Age of Jefferson* (New York, 1979), p. 30. For municipal elections, the same freehold requirements prevailed, but in 1804 those renters who paid a rent of at least $25 annually were also permitted the local franchise (ibid.; Sidney I. Pomerantz, *New York: An American City, 1783-1803* [New York, 1938], p. 72). Can any Latin Americanist imagine a panel of petty jurors selected for the Mayor's Court from among artisans, gentlemen, merchants, grocers, and others? See "A Panel of Petit Jurors to be Summoned to attend the Court of Common Pleas called the Mayor's Court," 14 July 1795, HDC, MC. My view of the personal wealth of the grocers is based on an analysis of the grocers resident in the First Ward in 1816 and 1821, and the Second and Sixth Wards in 1819 and 1821 (HDC, Jury lists and Tax Assessment Lists, 1816, 1819, 1821).

It is more difficult to determine the number of grocers and grocery stores in New York City than in many Spanish American cities because the New York grocers were not licensed.[6] However, a state law required that any person selling spiritous liquors in quantities smaller than five gallons had to obtain a license from the commissioner of excise. The Humane Society stated in 1810 that during the previous year some 1,800 licenses had been issued by the commissioner for the sale of spiritous liquors.[7] A recent estimate places the number of licenses granted to groceries for the sale of "strong drink" in 1811 at 1,300.[8] It is doubtful that there were as many as 1,300 grocery stores in the city at this time.[9] In English-speaking America many of the so-called groceries might better be referred to as groggeries;[10] that is, they were merely small drinking houses, some perhaps with food to sell.

It is also difficult to determine who among the grocers were wholesalers and who were retailers. Longworth's famous and much referred to *City-Directory* lists people alphabetically and does not always indicate occupation; the description "grocer," when included, does not indicate whether wholesale or retail.[11] It is sometimes possible to discern wholesalers from retailers through examination of inventories of grocers who died intestate, although some retailers may have had a larger and more varied inventory than some wholesalers. Thus, unlike Spanish America, a study of New York grocers must necessarily include wholesalers.

---

[6]The only occupational categories that required licenses from the city were the cartmen, porters, hackney coachmen, butchers, and tavern and inn keepers (Pomerantz, *New York*, pp. 464-68; Rock, *Artisans of the New Republic*, pp. 205-29; Eugene P. McParland, "The Socio-Economic Importance of the Tavern in New York During the British Period, 1664-1776" [MA thesis, Queens College, 1970], pp. 74-81).

[7]*New York Evening Post*, 9 January 1810.

[8]Rock, *Artisans of the New Republic*, p. 297.

[9]Even with 1,000 groceries, the store-to-population ratio in 1810, when the city's population was 96,000 (ibid., p. 14), would have been 1:96. This is nearly the same store-to-population ratio that prevailed in Buenos Aires in 1810, 1:94. However, as noted, the ratios for the other cities investigated were far greater, in the range of one to several hundred.

[10]See Gerald Carson's comment in *The Old Country Store* (New York, pb., 1965), pp. 13-14.

[11]Longworth's *American Almanac, New York Register, and City-Directory* (New York, by year).

A comparison of New York grocers with those of Spanish America suggests several interesting similarities. The New Yorkers faced many of the same problems confronting their Spanish American counterparts. For instance, although the New Yorkers sold both imported and locally produced items with few restrictions, they had to contend with competition from public markets; and there were restrictions against the purchase of market items for resale before the general population had sufficient time to purchase these in the markets.[12] And, not unexpectedly, there was a restriction against the sale of at least one item--in this case, fresh meat. This restriction placed the grocers at odds with another group of business people, the butchers; the two groups were involved in political in-fighting throughout the first decades of the nineteenth century.[13]

The inventories of the New York grocers seem not to have been as varied as those in Spanish America, although they may have been as large.[14] Perhaps this was because the New York grocers retailed more wine and hard liquor for consumption in the store than did Spanish

---

[12]Pomerantz, *New York*, pp. 176-77. These problems have some claim to universality; see Braudel, *Wheels of Commerce*, pp. 48-49. For a brief comment on the market as stimulator of business for fixed stores and on the fixed store as a competitor for the market, see Braudel, *Wheels of Fortune*, pp. 30, 60. For a fine study of the food marketing system in London during the seventeenth century, see Dorothy Davis, *A History of Shopping* (Toronto, 1966), pp. 72-99.

[13]MA, City Clerk, Box #2, Market Committee-Stalls & Licenses, Nov. 1812; Market Committee Reports, 1828. The grocers also had a problem over the Sabbath. Many wanted to remain open on Sunday, but a long public campaign against them eventually won out (MCC, vol. 7, pp. 72-73; City Clerk Filed Papers, Box #2 (Police Committee); MCC, vol. 17, pp. 5, 134-35, 206-7.

[14]For the period 1797-1830, the inventoried estates of 50 grocers have been found. Some examples of store inventories are HDC, Benjamin Sands, Inventory S-16; Henry T. Ramp (located between files R-3 and R-4); James McKeever, Inventory Mc-68; Harvey Buchanan, Inventory B-360; John N. Brower, Inventory B-305; Absalom Ferris, Inventory F-31; Patrick McCarty, Inventory Mc-19; Mathew Gillaspy, Inventory G-57. Of great interest is the Receipt Book of Nazareth B. Taylor, retail grocer, in New York Historical Society; and the Account Books of Dennis Doyle & Company, Manuscript Division, New York Public Library. For a discussion of what London grocers sold during the seventeenth century see Davis, *History of Shopping*, pp. 93-95. Interesting information on retail storekeeping is to be found in Lewis E. Atherton, *The Southern Country Store, 1800-1860* (Baton Rouge, 1949); and idem, *The Frontier Merchant in Mid-America* (Columbia, MO, 1971).

American grocers in such cities as Caracas, Puebla, and Mexico City. The New York grocers could do as much business selling fewer general store items but more wine and liquor.

Yet, the contents of the inventories were largely similar. Small retail grocery stores seem to have sold basically the same items, such as spices, chocolate, cheese, starch, rice, molasses, to mention only a few.

The New York grocers invested relatively little capital in the tools of the trade, such as store fixtures, showcases, counters, scales, weights and measures, and barrels.[15] The grocers of Mexico, on the other hand, invested heavily in such accoutrements. A New York grocer with the same investment as a Mexican might have maintained a substantially larger inventory.

An important difference between the grocers of Spanish America and New York is that the New Yorkers appear to have invested sizable amounts of money in income-producing limited liability instruments, such as bonds or bank notes, or in mortgages.[16] More banks and insurance companies operated in New York than in Spanish America. This difference between the two regions reflects a difference in their stages of economic development, perhaps owing to several decades of independence in the United States at the same time that colonial status prevailed in Spanish America. Spanish American grocers invested in additional stores simply because they lacked other opportunities for attractive, long-term income-producing ventures. It is conceivable that maturing capitalist economies display a propensity to withdraw entrepreneurial capital from the business cycle and place it in real property

---

[15]For examples of the relation between fixtures, showcases, etc., and inventory items, see the above-cited inventories of Ramp; McKeever; Buchanan; Brower; McCarty; Gillaspy; Ferris; and Benjamin Sands, HDC, Inventory S-16; William hall, Inventory H-18.

[16]See the examples of the above-cited Sands and Hall; and Sutton Craft, HDC, Inventory C-254; James Harris, Inventory H-69; and the intentions expressed in the wills of Henry Morgan, Patrick McClosky, and William Finch. Manuscript copies of the wills--few originals are extant--are in HDC, Liber 51, p. 185; Liber 56, pp. 20-24; Liber 57, p. 252. Many New York grocers also owned real estate. Examples drawn from wills may be seen in the following Libers in the HDC; 51, pp. 342-44; 47, pp. 41-45; 43, pp. 574-76, 414-16; 46, pp. 463-76; 55, pp. 256-61, 409-12, 583-85; 56, pp. 475-79, 154-59; 57, pp. 135-39; 59, pp. 422-25. Examples drawn from Conveyances of Deed are in the following Libers on microfilm at the OCR: 103, pp. 562-64, 634-36; 86, pp. 166-69; 137, pp. 216-18; 140, pp. 251-53, 253-55.

mortgages, government bonds, stocks, and the like.[17]   Certainly, investment of "surplus capital" or one's estate in such instruments (especially since limited liability became more widespread as the nineteenth century progressed) was an appropriate means of providing for one's future, for hedging against downturns in the economy, and for providing for one's family after one's demise, although this did remove capital from the active business cycle. Nonetheless, the different stages of economic maturity may have caused the Spanish American grocers to be, at times, more entrepreneurial than their northern counterparts.[18] For the Spanish Americans the choice was very much between more business--a larger store or an additional one--or investment in mortgages or land.

---

[17]Thus the existence of the East India Company enabled some Dutch Calvinists to retire "very early...from the brewing industry to live upon investments..." in the company (Miriam Beard, *A History of Business*, 2 vols. [Ann Arbor, pb., 1963], 1: 275). One of the rare possibilities for potentially long-term investment in a company in Spanish America was in the few maritime insurance companies that appeared toward the end of the colonial period. There were at least two in Mexico, one in Cuba, and one in Argentina, and perhaps others elsewhere. The organizational plan of the Argentine maritime insurance company "La Confianza" called for an issue of 400 shares at 1,000 pesos each (Enrique Wedovoy, *La evolución económica rioplatense a fines del siglo XVIII y principios del siglo XIX a la luz de la historia del seguro* [La Plata, 1962], pp. 222-25). For other investment possibilities, although not likely for small retail grocers, see Brading, *Miners and Merchants in Bourbon Mexico*, pp. 127, 297-98). It was not until the United States became independent that a broad array of long-term investment possibilities other than mortgages appeared. The first maritime insurance company was founded probably as late as 1757 (Herman E. Kroos and Charles Gilbert, *American Business History* [Englewood Cliffs, pb., 1972], p. 64). Between 1781 and 1830 there were many commercial banks, savings banks (as well as private banks), trust companies, general insurance companies, brokerage firms, and a profusion of stock-issuing manufacturing companies (Kroos and Gilbert, *American Business History*, p. 109). Not all of these would have been attractive to retail grocers when thinking of the future of their families. During the early nineteenth century the commercial banks paid dividends of 9 to 12 percent, but by the 1830s these were down to the 5 to 8 percent range. Furthermore, the first bank failure probably did not occur until 1809, but between that date and 1815, 208 banks failed (Kroos and Gilbert, *American Business History*, p. 115). Nevertheless, there were relatively safe dividend and interest-producing investment possibilities, including water companies, and as the decades progressed, municipal bonds.

[18]The evidence of 50 estate inventories and a greater number of wills suggests also that few New Yorkers were multiple store owners.

Mortgages did not provide daily sustenance from an inventory nor enough interest to support a family with only a few hundred or even 1,000 or 2,000 pesos to invest. Land may have been a plausible investment for someone with an agrarian background, but it was not a secure income-producing investment.

Appendix 1
Personal Profiles

A. SMALL RETAIL GROCERS IN MEXICO CITY, 1811-13

Between 1811 and 1813 a census of all residents of Mexico City was carried out, with results that illuminate the personal lives of the small retail grocers. The census was taken at the *cuartel menor* level and included only those people who actually lived in the cuartel menor. It recorded names of residents, place of origin, marital status, age, race, and in a general sense, occupation. This is significant information; yet the census has limitations. People in business were generically referred to as "Comerciantes," usually in abbreviation. Thus, it is not possible to differentiate roles within the broad commercial category. Since there were various and quite distinct levels of commercial activity in Mexico City during the era, with dozens of different kinds of stores, it will take many specific studies to realize the full potential of this census.

The Grocers of Cuartel Menor 1

With a population of 10,705 in 1811, cuartel menor 1 could have been a city itself.[1] Table 11 identifies 12 grocers as residents of this cuartel. The names of several other possible resident grocers were not included because information about them was too speculative. Further, both silent and active partners often were not enumerated in censuses.[2]

---

[1] AGNM, Ramo De Padrones, vol. 53, "Padron del quartel menor num 1 formado con arreglo al nuevo Reglamento de Policia de Agosto de este año...concluido en 30 de Dic. de 1811...."

[2] Others not identified are those who may have entered and departed a grocery business in a matter of months and whose presence among the grocers consequently may have gone unrecorded.

Table 11

GROCER RESIDENTS OF CUARTEL MENOR 1 IN 1811*

Name	Age	Marital Status	Race	Origin	# Children
1. Don Pedro Cortes	55	Widower	White	Mexico	1
2. Don Fernando Albear	45	Married	White	Spain	6
3. Don Juan Antonio Ruvín	50	Bachelor	White	Spain	-
4. Don José Pedraza	59	Married	White	Mexico	3
5. Don Miguel Cobacho	40	Married	White	Mexico	5
6. Don Manuel de la Torre	58	Married	White	Mexico	3
7. Don Fernando Hermosa	60	Married	White	Spain	2
8. Don Domingo Ugarte	60	Married	White	Spain	4
9. Don Domingo Ugarte y Hacha	44	Married	White	Spain	5
10. Don Antonio del Rio	29	Married	White	Mexico	0
11. Don Pedro Marcos Gutiérrez	47	Married	White	Spain	2
12. Don Andres de Aguayo	56	Married	White	Spain?	7

Note:
Don Domingo Ugarte was the uncle of Don Domingo Ugarte y Hacha. In the documents the Hacha (or Acha) is sometimes left out, and it becomes difficult, sometimes impossible, to distinguish between them.

*Source:
AGNM, Ramo De Padrones, vol. 53, "Padron del quartel menor num. 1 formado con arreglo al nuevo Reglamento de Policia de Agosto de este ano...concluido en 30 de Dic. de 1811...."

Thus, there were really more grocers than the couple of hundred who would appear periodically in the censuses. Nonetheless, of those couple of hundred officially counted as grocers, only 12 appear to have lived in cuartel menor 1. Why did so few grocers live where they owned stores? Perhaps too little housing was available.

The 12 identified grocers are not a sample--they are the ones who actually lived in cuartel menor 1 in 1811. When considered in relationship to the total number of grocers in Mexico City in that year, their numbers are statistically insignificant. Yet the census provides vital information that enhances the grocers' general profile.

Six grocers were from Spain and 5 were from Mexico.[3] Their ages ranged from 29 to 60, with a mean age of 48.5 years. Ten were married; 1 was a bachelor, although living with a widow; and 1 was a widower. The mean age of the 10 wives was 37.7 years.

The grocers of cuartel menor 1 tended to marry and to have children. It should be noted that the wives of 1811 might not have been first wives nor the mothers of the children listed in the census, which is vague on the matter. One of the Spanish grocers had a Spanish wife; the others presently had Mexican wives. All children were born in Mexico. Several of the men had much younger wives. One 60-year-old man had a 29-year-old wife and 7 children, the oldest being 18, obviously not hers; a 58-year-old man had a 29-year-old wife and 3 young children. The ages of several other men were within a few years of their wives' ages. Furthermore, 1 man had a wife a year older than he, and a second a concubine 2 years older. It is clear that some grocers began to produce children late in life. One 60-year-old had 2 children, ages 4 and 3. A 55-year-old widower had a 9-year-old child. A 58-year-old grocer had 3 children ranging in age from 2 to 12. A 45-year-old with a 31-year-old wife had 6 children ranging in age from 1 to 8.

Beyond this the census provides other information that is interesting. Some of the grocers were wealthy by any standards. Some not only had store employees but boarded them at home. And many had servants. This is not the profile of an impoverished group, but then these grocers certainly were not representative; they were the more successful ones. It is worthwhile to consider several of them individually.

---

[3]Everyone officially considered a grocer in this period was indeed that, but some may also have been owners of tiendas mestizas. The grocery store may only have been a minor part of a larger operation. Any of the grocers mentioned in this appendix may have been principally owners of tiendas mestizas, but what is certain is that to one degree or other they were owners of grocery stores.

Some suggestions about marriage patterns in Mexico City are presented in Silvia M. Arrom, "Marriage Patterns in Mexico City, 1811," *Journal of Family History* 3, no. 4 (winter 1978): 376-91.

110

Don Pedro Marcos Gutiérrez. Born in Spain, Gutiérrez in 1811 was 47 years old. He lived in house number 7, Calle del Empedradillo, cuartel menor 1--at the main plaza. It was on that street that he owned and operated a grocery store between 1806 and 1815. In 1816 his store was in the same building as the house in which he lived. The combined rental of the house and store in 1816 was 1,840 pesos.[4] A grocery store could have been established with less capital than these combined rents. By 1816 Gutiérrez had 2 nephews as partners in the store. Additionally, he had 2 employees that year who each earned 300 pesos annually.[5] Gutiérrez's Mexican wife was 40, and the pair had 2 children, a boy 11 and a girl 9. In 1811, 4 employees and 4 house guests resided with them. One of the house guests was a university graduate, and 2 were small- to middle-range agrarians. The fourth was a merchant. Gutiérrez also employed 8 servants.

Don Fernando Hermosa. Hermosa lived in house number 9, also on Calle del Empedradillo, but his store had earlier been located elsewhere; its location in 1811 in unclear. He was from Spain, 60 years of age, and had a Mexican wife, 40 years old. They had a 4-year-old son and a 3-year-old daughter. Living with them were 6 bachelor employees from Spain, 2 guests, and 11 servants.

Don Domingo Ugarte y Hacha. A slight possibility exists that this Don Domingo Ugarte was not a grocer, but the nature of his own store (a wine store) and his business relationship with his grocer nephew argue for inclusion here. He was a 44-year-old Spaniard with a 43-year-old Mexican wife. Together they had 5 children, ranging in age from 2 to 16. Living with them were 3 Spanish bachelor employees, 2 guests, and 11 servants (including 2 children).

Don Andrés de Aguayo. Aguayo was a 56-year-old Spaniard with a 29-year-old Mexican wife. They had 7 children, ranging in age from 1 to 18. Two were between 14 and 18 years of age, certainly not those of his wife. One guest and 4 servants lived with them.

Don José Pedraza. Pedraza was Mexican, 59, with a 44-year-old Mexican wife and 3 children, ranging in age from 10 to 19. Living with them were a young clerk and 4 servants.

---

[4]AHH, Consulados, Leg. 426-16, "Padrón General de los Comerciantes que abriga esta Capital en sus Ocho Quarteles mayores...."

[5]Ibid.

It seems clear that for some, at least, keeping a grocery store was profitable and contributed to a life style beyond what the grocers' traditional reputation would suggest possible. Not all grocers who lived in cuartel menor 1 were so affluent; 3 lived in apartments, and in total had only 3 servants (1 had none). Only 1 of them had a store employee living with him.

The Grocers of Cuartel Menor 5

Cuartel menor 5 was located in the center of the city. It comprised 15 blocks and held a population of 9,630 in 1811.[6] Seven, and possibly 4 other grocers, have been identified as having lived in the cuartel. One of the 7 was either Don Pedro Fuente or Don Pedro de la Fuente. The former was a 48-year-old Mexican widower, with 4 children ranging in age from 7 to 18. Two servants lived with them in an apartment. Don Pedro de la Fuente was also Mexican, 38, and a widower. He had 3 children, ranging in age from 8 to 18. The family lived in their "corner store." The Fuentes were so similar that either could be selected for this profile.

The 4 possible grocers were unremarkable in profile and fit in well with the others in this cuartel. One of them exemplifies the problems involved in securing hard information on storekeepers. In this cuartel menor lived three Don José Rodríguezes declared to be in the commercial world. One of them was a grocer. There was a 60-year-old Spanish bachelor with 2 servants. There was also a 45-year-old Mexican married to a 28-year-old Mexican. He had a young child and lived in first floor rooms. The third Rodríguez was a Mexican, 29, married, also with a young child. He lived in an apartment.

Eliminating Fuente, the remaining 6 grocers (including 1 woman) averaged 44.8 years in age, a few years younger than those in menor 1. Four of the 7 were from Spain and 3 were Mexican (both Fuentes were Mexican). There were 4 wives, all Mexican, with a mean age of 32.8 years, similarly younger than the wives of the menor 1 grocers.

The cuartel menor 5 grocers were noticeably less affluent than those of menor 1. One lived in a store; 2 lived in apartments; 1 lived in an accesoría; and 1 lived on a mezzanine. This was a modest residential pattern, yet these grocers were not necessarily impoverished. Don Juan Antonio Aristi, a Spaniard, 43, married to a Mexican, 29, had 7 children, ranging in age from 2 months to 12 years. Three bachelor Mexican employees, 2 young boys, and 7 servants lived with them. Don Domingo Llanos, a 46-year-old Spanish bachelor, living on a mezzanine, had so large a household that most of the residents probably were boarders rather

---

[6]AGNM, Ramo de Padrones, vol. 54, "Padron del Quartel Menor N. 5...dic. de 1811."

than guests. The remainder of the grocers in this group had 1 or 2 servants or none at all. They simply had not reached the level of success enjoyed by the grocers in menor 1. Further, this group of husbands and wives was younger than those in menor 1. Perhaps a few more years of enterprise would make a difference--but this is speculation.

One of those in the group of 7 in menor 5 was especially interesting. Doña María Zepeda was a Mexican widow, 47, owner of a grocery store in 1811. (During the same year the store was also listed as a wine store, but this in 1811 was probably as much a matter of nomenclature as substantive difference between store categories.) In the same year Doña María lived in an accesoría. With her lived a 21-year-old bachelor clerk, also Mexican; a 65-year-old widowed seamstress, perhaps a boarder; and one 20-year-old female servant. Not affluent, she nonetheless managed to remain in business for a few years: in 1815 she had a grocery store at the same address as her 1811 store.[7]

This profile of the small retail grocers of Mexico City is enriched by the example of one further personality. Don José Xaraba was born in Mexico City. He married 3 times, and when he died in 1797, he was survived by 3 children. The eldest was more than 25 years of age, the youngest just 3 months old.[8] Neither of the first 2 wives brought anything of economic value to the marriages. To his first marriage, Xaraba brought 2 stores (they would be and perhaps were then grocery stores) in which he had invested some 4,000 pesos. During this marriage, his principal increased to about 14,000 pesos. By the time of the third marriage, Xaraba possessed 3 grocery stores, which he owned at the time of his death. His principal at the time of the third marriage was down to about 6,000 pesos, the wife bringing to the marriage about 300 pesos. After his death, inventories were taken of the 3 grocery stores. Their values (including aperos and pawns) were 1,114 pesos, 534 pesos, and 1,060 pesos.[9] All collateral information suggests that these were three successful grocery stores, yet they were modest in capitalization.

In 1797 Xaraba owned a piece of property (including a house) for which he had borrowed a considerable amount of money. When he wrote his will he owed 8,030 pesos, perhaps the cost of the property. To three people, one a *marqués*, the second a merchant, and the third a priest, he owed 2,000 pesos each. The remaining 2,030 pesos he owed to a grocery store for which he held power of attorney. It is unusual that a grocer should have been able to purchase a property worth more than his 3

---

[7]Doña María Zepeda was sometimes listed in documents as Doña María Josefa Zepeda.

[8]AGNM, Consulados, Tomo 160, "Ynbentarios formados por muerte del Sargento Don José Xaraba."

[9]Ibid.

grocery stores put together. Furthermore, it is interesting that a grocer should have been able to withdraw more than 2,000 pesos from any grocery store, especially one over which he held power of attorney.

It is possible that Xaraba purchased his house in 1796 or in early 1797. In November 1796 a Maestro Mayor of Architecture evaluated a house that may have been the one that Xaraba purchased. The evaluation was filed with other papers relating to his estate, a strong indication that he had purchased the house. The total value of the house was put at 9,100 pesos, just about what Xaraba owed in 1797. The house possessed 5 accesorías facing on one street and 7 accesorías facing on a second street. There was also a corner accesoría that served as a store. This one had 4 doors, a backroom, and a patio with a hut used to store charcoal. Another accesoría and additional rooms completed this large and expensive house.

Beyond this, the information included in the papers relating to Xaraba's estate is detailed and informative. At his death, an inventory was taken of Xaraba's personal possessions, including his books. There was an air of sumptuousness about it. The inventory of books shows 53 separate entries; several of the books were of 2 volumes, and one was of 12 volumes. Most of the books were religious in nature, something to be expected of a library in a society whose culture was so extensively dominated by the Church, but there were also books about war, geography, legislation, and cooking. Xaraba had several volumes of the *Gaceta de México*. The total value of the library was put at 47 pesos, in itself a substantial sum.[10]

---

[10]The library inventory is in ibid. For a large and impressive personal inventory of an Argentine grocer, see AGNA, Registro de Escribano 3, 1789, Will of Don Ramón Maseira, 14 March 1789. There is very little information in the documents about personal property of either the pulperos or bodegueros of Caracas. Don Guillermo Morales was a partner in a small pulpería. He possessed, among other things, some household items, a bed, a dozen small chairs, 5 place settings of silver (RP, Escribanías, 1813 [Aramburu], ff. 62-65, Will of Don Guillermo Morales, 1 June 1813). Another pulpero had a dozen and a half place settings, his personal clothing and furniture, and some other fairly valuable items (ibid., 1802 [Aramburu], ff. 494-97, Will of Don José Francisco Trugillo, 22 Oct. 1802). One had a watch among his apparently few possessions (ibid., ff. 263-64, Will of Don Domingo Gonzales Garrido, 4 Dec. 1802). A fourth had a few personal items, including " a set of gold buttons worth 30 pesos (ibid., ff. 212-15, Will of Don Juan García de la Cruz, 26 May 1802). It is interesting that these 4 pulperos were from the Canary Islands. Perhaps they were more inclined to list personal items in a will than were the Venezuelans. In any event, it is likely that most pulperos possessed more personal items than one might infer from the wills. Inventories of those who died intestate have not helped clarify this issue. The Caracas Testamentarias are in RP.

Xaraba's house seems to have been well furnished. There were several dozen chairs, some of fine wood, some with straw backing. The household inventory comprised 77 separate entries, with a total value of 196 pesos. Most of the items were not relatively costly. For instance, 2 tables were valued together at only 2 pesos. The dozen fine wood chairs were valued at under 5 pesos.

Rather more remarkable, perhaps, was Xaraba's personal wardrobe, which received 28 separate entries, assessed in total at 145 pesos. Xaraba owned so many coats of all descriptions that he might have opened a clothing store. One outfit was valued at 30 pesos and probably was his militia uniform: he was a sergeant in the Urban Regiment of Commerce. His wife had personal possessions valued at 196 pesos. In total, items within the house were valued at 544 pesos, the worth of one of his grocery stores.

B. THE BUENOS AIRES GROCERS IN 1778

According to the census of 1778 there were 194 small retail grocers in Buenos Aires in that year.[11] The census presents valuable information: place of residence; age; marital status; number of children, slaves, servants, and people residing with the family or the head of the household. However, there are several weaknesses in the census. As Lyman L. Johnson has observed, not every resident was identified by occupation. There is information concerning home ownership, although this was not a priority of the census, but the enumerators in different parts of the city took varying degrees of interest in the matter. Furthermore, while there is racial identification, it is vague and misleading.[12]

It is sometimes assumed that wealth contributes to an ability or willingness to marry, and perhaps this is borne out in the case of the artisans through the example of the silversmiths (Figure 5). However,

---

[11]Padrón de 1778.

[12]Johnson, "Artisans of Buenos Aires," p. 153 n.14. The note about the misleading nature of the census is my own. There were free blacks in Buenos Aires, and it is surprising that more were not pulperos in 1778. For the number of free blacks in the city during the early nineteenth century and for some observations on discrimination toward them, see George R. Andrews, *The Afro-Argentines of Buenos Aires, 1800-1900* (Madison, 1980), pp. 39-41, 45-47.

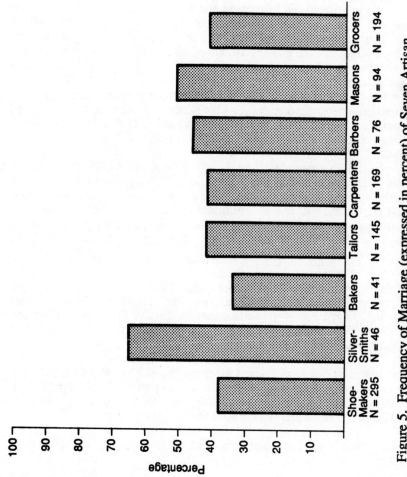

Figure 5. Frequency of Marriage (expressed in percent) of Seven Artisan Groups and the Grocers of Buenos Aires in 1778-1780.

bakers were often wealthy when compared to other artisans, yet not as many were married in the 1778-80 period. A majority of the married bakers were over 40, which may suggest, as Lyman L. Johnson has observed, "that bakers deferred marriage until they were well established in the trade and were able to provide adequately for a family."[13] The example of the city's wholesale import-export merchants, the city's richest and most prestigious group of business people, suggests a relationship between wealth and marriage. In 1778 there were 145 wholesale import-export merchants in Buenos Aires, and 76 percent were married.[14] At the same time, 42.3 percent of the grocers were married.[15]

A majority of the merchants and grocers were married to younger women in 1778. In that year there were 111 merchant couples and 67 grocer couples present in the city.[16] Fifty-six percent of the merchants and 53.7 percent of the grocers had wives between 5 and 14 years younger than themselves. Twenty-four percent of the merchants and 22.4 percent of the grocers were more than 15 years older than their wives. Fifteen percent of the merchants and 20.9 percent of the grocers married women of approximately their own ages. Five percent of the merchants married older women, as did 2.9 percent of the grocers.[17] The mean age of the 67 married grocers in 1778 was 39.2 years; the mean age of their wives was 28.8 years.

Eighty-five percent of the 67 grocer couples of 1778 had children. Of the 15 percent who did not have children, 6 couples had the reason of either being too old or too young. One couple's ages, for instance, were 62 and 60; another 40 and 16. Furthermore, the census of 1778 does not indicate whether a childless couple was only apparently so, that is, whether older children lived away from the parental domicile.

---

[13]Johnson, "Artisans of Buenos Aires," pp. 204-5. For a discussion of the relationship between economics, race, sex, and marital status, see Michael M. Swann, *Tierra Adentro: Settlement and Society in Colonial Durango* (Boulder, 1982), pp. 225-26; and on the relationship between race and socioeconomic status, ibid., p. 248.

[14]Socolow, *Merchants of Buenos Aires* pp. 15, 37. Not all of the 145 may have been involved in both importing and exporting (ibid., pp. 54-55). Twelve percent of the merchants married before the age of 25 (ibid., p. 40). I do not have similar information for the grocers.

[15]Padrón de 1778. The number of married grocers may be off plus or minus 2.

[16]The merchant statistic is from Socolow, *Merchants of Buenos Aires*, p. 40. The grocer statistic was extrapolated from the Padrón de 1778.

[17]Ibid.

Eliminating the 6 couples who perhaps for the reason of age were childless in 1778 raises the percentage of grocer couples with children to 93.4. The average number of children per grocer couple with children was 3.4.[18] Fifteen couples had a least 5 children each.[19]

Slave Ownership

Perhaps more than marriage, slave ownership is an indication of wealth. Thirty-two percent of all those people engaged in commerce and 100 percent of the large-scale wholesale import-export merchants owned slaves in 1778 (Figure 6). Approximately one-quarter of the bakers (24.4 percent) and silversmiths (28.3 percent) owned slaves, while only 14.4 percent of the grocers did.[20]

That all of the wealthiest merchants in Buenos Aires in 1778 should have owned slaves is not surprising. That more silversmiths owned slaves than did bakers is interesting since silversmiths had recourse to apprentices, while bakers customarily took advantage of slave labor. In fact, those bakers who did own slaves owned on average more slaves than did the silversmiths who were slave owners. Additionally, more of the baker-owned slaves were male,[21] an indication that they were used in the

---

[18]There were also 5 widowers with children. The ages of the widowers ranged from 51 to 70, and on average they had 3.8 children.

[19]These figures have been extrapolated from the Padrón de 1778. From an international perspective, the average number of children per grocer couple in Buenos Aires was high (see Peter Laslett, ed., *Household and Family in Past Time* [Cambridge, Eng., pb., 1974], pp. 59, 61, 126). José Luis Moreno has estimated the average number of children per family in Buenos Aires according to occupation. The numbers run from 3.8 among the higher status families to 2.4 among the lower ("La estructura social y demográfica de la ciudad de Buenos Aires en el año de 1778," *Anuario del Instituto de Investigaciones Históricas* [Universidad del Litoral, Rosario, Arg., 1965], pp. 151-70). According to these estimates the grocers ranked high up the scale of occupation status. See also Swann, *Tierra Adentro*, pp. 247-57.

[20]The 32 percent figure and the merchant information are from Socolow, *Merchants of Buenos Aires*, p. 77. She does not specify the number of large-scale import-export merchants in this instance. The artisan information is from Johnson, "Artisans of Buenos Aires," pp. 155, 206. The grocer information is from the Padrón de 1778.

[21]Johnson, "Artisans of Buenos Aires," p. 206. And, as Johnson points out, some people enumerated as bakers may have been employees and

business. That relatively fewer grocers owned slaves than the other groups mentioned may be a reflection of their lesser wealth, but this may also be a reflection of the availability of cheap hired labor and the presence of children and spouses capable of working in the store. However, there is still a significant difference between the 32 percent slave ownership for all those engaged in commerce and the 14.4 percent for the grocers.

Nonetheless, some grocers were affluent. One owned 5 slaves; 2 owned 6 slaves each, and 1 grocer owned 8 slaves. Susan Socolow has pointed out that there were merchants who did not own slaves, but these were young men, often recent arrivals to Buenos Aires.[22] The older, more established merchants owned slaves. Age was not a factor in slave ownership among the grocers. Eighty-four of the 194 grocers in Buenos Aires in 1778 were 35 years of age or older and were not slave owners.[23]

therefore not likely to have been in a position to own slaves. See also Moreno, "Estructura social y demográfica," pp. 151-70.

[22]Socolow, *Merchants of Buenos Aires*, p. 77.

[23]Padrón de 1778.

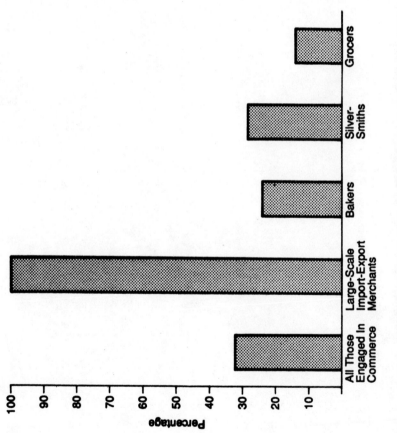

Figure 6. Selected Occupations as Slaveowners in Buenos Aires in 1778.

Appendix 2
The Pulperos of Caracas
in 1816: A Microview

In 1816 officials of the royal treasury prepared a census of all pulperías in Caracas for the purpose of managing the collection of the sales tax--the famous alcabala.[1] The resulting census of 1816 is informative and permits an intimate view of the pulperos and their pulperías during a relatively brief period.

The alcabala was not an accurate measure of retail sales activity. Theoretically levied on most goods each time they were sold, the tax was transferred from Spain to the Indies at the end of the sixteenth century.[2] Until 1636 the alcabala rate was 2 percent, when it was doubled for New Spain. It has not been possible to determine the rate for Caracas, but perhaps it was 3 or 4 percent. As in many other parts of the Spanish world, the Caracas storekeeper was assessed a single sum, payable by installment. The assessment was merely an estimate, and in Caracas it was not altered annually, nor upon the sale or purchase of a store. Thus the assessment did not necessarily reflect current business activity. Some items a grocer might carry were not subject, according to Haring, to the alcabala, perhaps most importantly bread.[3]

One hundred twelve different pulpería operations (some succeeded others in the same venue) functioned in Caracas in 1816. They were assessed at a mean of 27.1 pesos for the year (mean deviation = 4.2).[4]

---

[1] AGNV, Real Hacienda, vol. 2423, "Año de 1816, Recept*. Admon. de Alcabalas de Caracas, Quaderno de Pulperías." References to 1816 in this appendix are from this census.

[2] Haring, *Spanish Empire in America*, pp. 268-70.

[3] Ibid.

[4] The assessments were in whole peso amounts rather than pesos and reales. Therefore the figures presented in this appendix are decimal figures rather than fractions of 8 reales per peso.

Eleven stores were assessed at the lowest figure of 18 pesos. One was assessed at 48 and another 42 pesos. Forty-five stores were assessed in the 20-peso range. Fifty-five of the pulperías were assessed at 30 or more pesos.

The census of 1816 lists a name (infrequently 2) for each pulpería, but not necessarily that of the owner. Thus, Don Fermin Hernández is listed for a pulpería on the corner of la Glorieta street. Appended information indicates that he was administering the store for Doña María Petronila Porras and her daughters. On 31 January he informed the royal treasury that he would no longer continue in that capacity. It has not been possible to determine how many other names belong to administrators, nor can it be discerned from this list, except in isolated cases, which pulperos had partners.

Another seemingly straightforward characteristic of the 1816 census is troublesome; not every person was enumerated with the honorific Don or Doña. Those without the honorific, one would presume, were *pardos*, that is, free people of color.[5] However, the Caracas census takers were not always fastidious. Apart from the random errors, officials employed differing approaches to enumeration. Thus, in the census of 1818 for Caracas, one cuartel employed the honorific and another did not use it at all.[6] The possibility exists that some of those Caracas pulperos of 1816 enumerated without the honorific were white--probably illegitimate and poor. The pardo classification has been used in this essay for those untitled pulperos in the 1816 list, but it has not been possible to demonstrate conclusively that all were indeed pardos. In the best Caracas census material whites have the don title and pardos do not. In this study the royal treasury officials have been given a large benefit of doubt.

---

[5]Unlike some parts of Spanish America, Indians are not involved in the controversy over don usage in Caracas. This was probably due to their comparatively insignificant numbers. See the population figures by sex and race for the early nineteenth century in John V. Lombardi, *People and Places in Colonial Venezuela* (Bloomington, 1976), pp. 183-85. For an excellent discussion of the pardo, see ibid., pp. 42-45. See also Verena Martínez-Alier, *Marriage, Class and Colour in Nineteenth-Century Cuba* (Cambridge, Eng., 1974), pp. 74, 83.

[6]ACM, Capitulares, vol. 2 (1818), ff. 37-92, Padrón of 1818. Ann Twinam has observed that by the eighteenth century in Medellín, any "male who was white and legitimate expected to be greeted" with the honorific don. "Medillinenses were scrupulous and consistent in the use of this title" ("Miners, Merchants, and Farmers," p. 230).

Of the 109 pulperos who operated the 112 pulperías,[7] there appear to have been 14 pardos and 1 parda. The 14 pardos were assessed at 28.3 pesos per year (mean deviation = 4.5), slightly higher than the general mean. The parda was assessed at 18 pesos. There were 10 white pulperas (owning 11 stores, assessed an average of 26.2 pesos, with a mean deviation of 4.2). During the course of the year, and including all pulperos and pulperías listed, 3 pardos sold their stores: 2 sold to whites and 1 to another pardo. Overall, 25 pulperías closed; it is not possible to determine when in all cases; some almost certainly closed in 1815. Two stayed open for a period of months in 1816 and are included among the 112. Three pardos and 1 parda closed their doors.[8]

There were also pardo bodegueros. In 1809, for instance, at the time of the visita of that year there were 82 bodegueros and 85 bodegas in Caracas. It appears that 10 of the 82 bodegueros were pardos.[9]

One further characteristic of the 1816 census is significant: beneath most of the names is an appended comment, seemingly made by more than 1 person. Many of these comments are unremarkable, indicating generally what was owed toward the alcabala assessment, and often a raise in the assessment. Of the 112 pulpería operations, 25 assessments were increased, with a mean raise of 5.5 pesos (mean deviation = 1.8). Beyond this the appended information is both interesting and deceptive; few historians would likely draw similar inferences on all matters.

The year 1816 was not extraordinary in Venezuelan history. No earthquake occurred, as did in 1812, nor change of military and political control in Caracas, as occurred earlier and would occur later.[10] Yet there were demographic alterations in Caracas during the independence period, and an unknown number of grocers fled during these years. The affluent

---

[7]The pulpero population has been arrived at on the basis of 1 name per store. This is because only 3 stores had partners listed, while many others had both unlisted active and inactive partners. The 109 figure is the minimum number of pulperos in 1816.

[8]It would be interesting to know whether pardos had difficulty establishing themselves in the more desirable areas. The addresses of the pulperías are listed, but the problem is that our knowledge of the Caracas urban economic and social topography is too crude to allow us to judge the better locations.

[9]Visitas, 1809.

[10]However, Don José Antonio Martines's pulpería was "sacked" in 1814, and, being unable to purchase a new inventory, he eventually had to close his store (AGNV, Real Hacienda, vol. 2423, "Año de 1816...Quaderno de Pulperías").

pulpero, Don Bartolomé Sotomayor, fled in 1813 to escape Bolívar's forces.[11] Don José María Camacho was a bodeguero who fled, leaving his store in someone's care. Shortly, Camacho's wife attempted to sell the store and had to appeal to the government to establish ownership.[12] These examples suggest that some stores were sold during this period when they might not have been sold under normal circumstances. Nevertheless, the trends suggested by the activities of the pulperos in 1816 are observable over many decades.

At least 36 pulperos (some may have been administrators) were in business more than 1 year, some many years. Pulperos sometimes fell out of the ranks or moved up to the bodeguero category only to become pulperos at a later date. Thus, Don Miguel Amaral was a pulpero at least in 1804, 1808, and 1809.[13] On 2 January 1816 he returned his pulpería license because "of many setbacks and illnesses."[14] However, he continued in the same location with a *bodegón*, waiting for his situation to improve. Unlike bodegas, the bodegones appear to have been small wholesale warehouses. In 1818 Amaral, then 60, was once again listed as a pulpero.[15] Don José Antonio Pino also converted his pulpería to a bodegón for the same reason. Sometimes the change in legal status was more fortunate. Don Antonio Medrade changed his pulpería into a bodega.[16] Don Pedro Manuel Pérez returned his pulpería license because he was no longer interested in running such a store. Instead, he placed a tobacco store in the same location.

---

[11]RP, Escribanía, 1815 (Correa), ff. 97-100, 101-7. Don José Hernández de Orta, isleño, was the owner of at least 2 tiendas de mercería between 1797 and 1802. He fled during the independence period to San Juan, where he also operated a tienda de mercería (AGPR, PN, Caja 446, ff. 49-51).

[12]Ibid.

[13]Visitas.

[14]AGNV, Real Hacienda, vol. 2423, "Año de 1816...Quaderno de Pulperías."

[15]ACM, Capitulares, vol. 2 (1818) ff. 37-92, Padrón of 1818.

[16]There were several "mixed pulperías" and "pulperías con bodega," a blurring of legal categories. Doña Romalda Ruvi had a "Pulpª Mestixa con Bodega." The document clearly states Bodega and not Bodegón. However, I am certain this is an error in the appended material, and should read Bodegón. In 1813 Don Sebastian Tovar owned a "Bodega y pulpería," presumably 2 different stores (RP, Escribanías, 1813 [Aramburu], ff. 27-30, Will of Don Sebastian Tovar, 5 March 1813).

Pulperías sometimes disappeared from the ranks because they were absorbed by other stores. Early in 1816 Salvador Flores closed his pulpería and transferred its effects to the pulpería belonging to Don Antonio Suárez, whom he had joined as a partner. Don José Delgado purchased a pulpería from Don Miguel Nuñes and removed the inventory to his own bodega. Don Vicente Ramos bought a pulpería from Don Domingo Henríquez and moved the stock to his own store, which he had purchased earlier in the year. Don Bernardo Valdés transferred the inventory of one pulpería to another.

Prospects sometimes seemed better than reality. Don Salvador Castillo purchased a pulpería from Don Luis Reveson on 13 February, "from which date he kept it closed for not having anything with which to stock it."[17]

There were indeed many closings. Don Blas Alfonso bought his pulpería around 15 May and closed it for having "nothing to sell." It had been purchased earlier in the year from Doña María Petronila Porras by Don Juan Rodríguez Marrero. Don Juan Manuel Alvarez closed his pulpería "for having nothing to sell in it, and nothing with which to stock it." María Agustina Arroya returned her license, "for having consumed the store's small capital due to her illnesses, and because she had nothing with which to continue in the store." Don Francisco García got sick and closed his store. Don José de la Rosa Hernández closed his store "because its principal was too limited." Don Gabriel Hidalgo went bankrupt. No one knew of his whereabouts. The treasury officials had it on good report that Don José María Sánchez closed his pulpería because he had lost his capital. Don Juan Vizente León closed his "because he had no principal." Pedro Morín returned his license "for having nothing to sell." Pedro Romero became sick and died. His widow, Paula Ponce, closed the pulpería because the store's small principal had been expended and nothing remained for restocking. Don Gregorio López moved his pulpería from the corner of Arrazolas to the corner of el Sordo. However, after the move no one knew anything of him and the store never opened. Nor did anyone know the whereabouts of Don Francisco Sambrano. The officials learned from neighbors that Sambrano had opened a very poorly supplied store and in a few days closed it. No one knew where Don Juan Marcos Gonzales was. Don José Gonzales Borges returned his license on 3 January, having closed his pulpería in December.

Partners were sometimes added. Don Isidro García joined Don José Martín Yanes, contributing 600 pesos in principal to the functioning pulpería, which had been purchased earlier in the year and then moved. Manual Peña purchased a pulpería from José Antonio Romero. Don Juan Mérida joined him for one-half the profits and an investment of 50 pesos. Later in the year Mérida sold out to Peña. Don Pedro López bought out

---

[17]But a Don Salvador del Castillo became a partner of Don Pedro Reyes on 30 October.

Doña Josefa Herrera's share of their pulpería. Don Antonio Guzmán
bought a pulpería and was joined in partnership by Don Salvador Pérez,
who invested 232 pesos. Don Antonio Pérez Guzmán purchased a
pulpería and Don Juan Saldivia joined him in partnership with a 100-peso
investment. Don José María Delgado took in 2 partners for one-fourth the
profits and no investment. Don Marcos Roxas took in Bernabe Roxas at
one-half the profits.[18]
     The degree to which the Caracas grocers were actively engaged in
the economy is revealed vividly by their purchases and sales of pulperías
(Table 12). Don Juan Rodríguez Marrero purchased his store from Doña
María Petronila Porras and sold it to Don Blas Alfonso, who closed it.
Don Juan José Marrero bought his store from Don Antonio Gonzales, who
had earlier bought his from Don Francisco Avila, and sold it to Don
Antonio Pérez Guzmán in less than 4 months. Marrero later repurchased
the store from Pérez and in about 3 months sold it to Don Francisco
Manuel Toledo. This all occurred in 1816. Don Bernardo Valdés moved
his pulpería from the Anauco Bridge to the corner of los Miracielos. Don
José Figueroa bought the one at Miracielos from Valdés and moved his
pulpería at Narauli to the new one. Soon Don Francisco Pellicer joined
Figueroa in partnership, and not long after that the two sold the store to
Don Andrés León and Don Juan Saldivia. Earlier in the year a Don
Andrés León had sold a pulpería (with a different address) to Don Juan
Brcijo, who within 2 months resold it. Don Miguel Nuñes bought a
pulpería from Don Miguel Gil, who sold it about 3 months later to Don
José Delgado. Don Feliciano González purchased a pulpería from Don
Juan Mérida and sold it to Don Antonio Guzmán within 3 months.
Guzmán took in a partner and then sold the store to Doña Inés María Soto.
González bought another pulpería.[19]

---

[18]With the same name, one would suspect a relative. Perhaps it was so
obvious that Bernabe Roxas was white that the official left the don out of
the appended information. However, he may have been a colored relative.

[19]Since the information about purchases and sales comes from the notices
of *avaluos de compra* or *venta*, which were generally presented to the
officials within a short time (apparently within 1 to 3 weeks normally) of
the transaction, the length of time the pulperías were held can only be
approximated. Those stores purchased and resold were held between 1
and 6 months. Six were held less than 4 months. Overall, 24 pulperías
were bought and not resold during 1816.

127

Table 12

PURCHASES AND SALES OF CARACAS PULPERIAS IN 1816*

Purchaser	From	To	Approximate Period Store Held
1.ᵃ Don Juan Rodríguez	Doña María Petronila Porras	Don Blas Alfonso	4.5 months (Alfonso closed it)
2. Don Antonio Gonzales	Don Francisco Avila	Don Juan José Marrero	3 months
Don Juan José Marrero	Don Antonio Gonzales	Don Antonio Pérez Guzmán	< 4 months
Don Juan José Marrero	Don Antonio Pérez Guzmán	Don Francisco Manuel Toledo	3 months
3. Don José Figueroa & & Don Francisco Pellicer	Don José Bernardo Valdés	Don Andrés León	5 months
4. Don Juan Brcijo	Don Andrés León	Don Marcos Machado	1-2 months
5. Don Miguel Nuñes	Don Miguel Gil	Don José Delgado	3 months (joins Delgado's bodega)
6. Doña María Josefa Herrera	Don Juan Pellicer	Don Pedro López (partner)	6 months
7. Don Feliciano González	Don Juan Mérida	Don Antonio Guzmán	3 months
Don Antonio Guzmán	Don Feliciano Gonzalez	Doña Inés Soto	4 months
8. Manuel Ponte	Doña Pilar Véliz	Don Feliciano Gonzalez	1 month (González holds onto this one)
9. Manuel García	Nicolás Gonzales	Don Francisco Pellicer	4 months
10. Doña Fernanda Bermejo	Don Manuel Guzmán (partner)	Don José ? & Don Rafael Barbuena	4 months

ᵃEach number indicates a single pulperia venue. This table includes 2 transactions between partners.

*Source:

AGNV, Real Hacienda, vol. 2423, "Ano de 1816, Receptª. Admon de Alcabalas de Caracas, Quaderno de Pulperías."

Appendix 3
The Mexico City Grocers as Real Property Owners

It is interesting to find storekeepers as owners of real property, the more so when they were small storekeepers, business people of relatively limited means when compared to the larger retailers and wholesalers. A storekeeper might purchase real property for a variety of reasons: to secure an estate for one's heirs; to add income-producing property to one's portfolio; to provide an outlet for excess cash; or to use the property as collateral for a loan. Capital that might have been employed to expand an inventory, to enlarge a store, or to acquire an additional store was sometimes dedicated to the purchase of a personal dwelling or an income-producing property. Furthermore, during most of the period 1750-1850 grocers were not incorporated; they were responsible for their business debts to the full extent of their personal property, and real property could be confiscated to resolve a business liability.[1]

In 1813 government officials carried out an extensive census of all dwellings in Mexico City to determine the amount of rent produced by each so that 10 percent could be deducted as a tax for the public treasury.[2]

---

[1] Spanish commercial law stipulated that in general all parties to a partnership were liable for debts to the full extent of their personal assets now and in the future (*Ordenanzas de Bilbao ... 1737* [many editions], Capítulo 10, Num. 13). There was a provision in the commercial code for a silent partner, the *socio comandita*, to have limited liability. According to Socolow (*Merchants of Buenos Aires*, p. 211), this form of partnership does not seem to have been in much use by the eighteenth century. It was in use in San Juan during the nineteenth century (Jay Kinsbruner, "The Pulperos of Caracas and San Juan during the First Half of the Nineteenth Century," *LARR* 13, no. 1 (1978): 65-85).

[2] *Padrón General De Las Casas Que Comprehenden Los Ocho Quarteles Mayores En Que Está Distribuida Esta Capital...1813* (Mexico City, 1903). The census does not treat *solares*; it only treats dwellings. A few

The rents were compared to those of 1796. Even if the owner lived in the dwelling a rent was stipulated for the purpose of collecting the treasury tax. While useful, the census, published in 1903, lacks refinement. For instance, owners were listed but not their occupations. It is simple to determine what the Church or titled nobility owned, but there is nothing in the census to indicate what the grocers, or the carpenters, or silversmiths, or others owned. Fortunately, the 1813 census is precisely in that period for which extensive information on the identities of the grocers has been gathered during this investigation. Unfortunately, it is not possible to consider the grocers within the context of other small- and middle-range storekeepers, since it is as yet impossible to identify the others in the census.

Several general characteristics of real property ownership in Mexico City are discernible from the 1813 census. The Church, the nobility, and women owned a great amount of property.[3]   Many

---

dwellings lack information, but this does not affect the pulperos. For a brief discussion of the nomenclature used in the census, see Rosa María Sánchez de Tagle, "Elements for the Analysis of the Internal Structure of Mexico City: A Typology of Dwellings," *LARR* 10, no. 2 (Summer 1975): 121-22.

Several Caracas grocers also owned real property. In 1807 Don Francisco de León, owner of a half-interest in a pulpería, owned 7 houses, 2 little stores, and 2 lots. He also owned 7 slaves (RP, *Escribanías*, 1807 (Texera), Will of Don Francisco de León, 18 Aug. 1807.) The lots may not have been very valuable. By 1807 lots in Caracas could be very small, and the municipal government had granted hundreds of them to poor residents free of charge (Waldron, "Social History," p. 156). Don Juan Pérez García owned a pulpería in 1765. By that date he had purchased about 32 acres of rural land for 100 pesos. Since his pulpería was valued at only 290 pesos, one wonders what motivated him toward purchasing land rather than increasing the inventory of a very modest grocery store (RP, *Escribanías*, 1765 [Therreros], ff. 185-89, Will of Don Juan Peres García, 22 Dec. 1765). Don Bartolomé Reyes owned a pulpería in 1820 that had a capitalization, by his estimate, of only 200 or 300 pesos. He also owned some rural land, 13 slaves, and almost 130 animals (Ibid., 1820 [Texera], ff. 165-68, Will of Don Bartolomé Reyes, 16 July 1820). Don Domingo Rodríguez Fuentes owned a pulpería in 1797 valued at 970 pesos, of which 600 pesos comprised his investment. He also owned 11 houses, 2 lots, 9 slaves, and some animals. Further, he had 1,200 pesos in cash on hand (Ibid., 1797 [Aramburu], ff. 57-62, Will of Don Domingo Rodríguez Fuentes, 5 July 1797).

[3]For information on Church ownership of real property in Mexico City in 1860, including a spatial representation of that ownership, see Carmen Morales, "Propiedad urbana de las corporaciones religiosas," in

individuals owned multiple-dwellings. For instance, the Marquesado del Valle owned all 6 houses on the extremely valuable Calle 1ª. de Plateros facing south. In 1813 these houses produced a rent of over 6,000 pesos. Del Valle also owned all 6 houses on Calle del Empedradillo (east), which produced an income that year of more than 8,000 pesos, and all 6 houses on the second street of Plateros, facing south, which produced a rental income of almost 6,000 pesos. Don Esteban Escalante owned all 15 houses on Calle de Celaya, south, bringing a rental of over 4,000 pesos.

Judging from the rentals, houses that were worth a great deal were frequently located on the same street as houses that were worth far less. For instance, the same Escalante owned houses on Celaya that rented for 768, 378, 366, and 324 pesos--but also for 96 pesos. On the street of the Quadrante de Santa Catalina, south, there were houses that rented for more than 1,200 pesos and more than 800 pesos. There was also a house that rented in total for less than 200 pesos. On nearby Tenexpam, north, there was a house that belonged to the Archbishopric that supposedly produced a rent of 1,980 pesos, a house that produced a rent of 360 pesos, and one that produced only 75 pesos. There are scores of similar examples. This evident intermingling of property values means that the small retail grocers were financially able to live throughout the city and on most of its streets.

Property ownership in 1813 was broadly based. On Calle de la Pila de Havana, south, María Gertrudis, "the fruit seller," owned an accesoría. So, too, did José "the sweets seller." Manuel "the carpenter" owned a house on that street. The rentals were 27, 15, and 18 pesos, respectively. At the Plazuela del Pradito, María India owned a house with a rental estimated at 6 pesos, and so too did the Indian Dolores. Clearly, there was a tendency toward real property ownership among all classes in Mexico City.

Fifteen grocers who almost certainly owned real property in 1813 have been identified (Table 13). No perfectly hard proof exists to warrant the inclusion of any of the grocers within this group. Most of the 15 owned at least 1 piece of real property on the same street as their grocery stores. In certain instances an unusual name was convincing; for example, included was the grocer Don José Montes de Oca, whose real property was not situated near his store. Since the goal of this essay is a general picture of the grocers as real property owners, included among the 15 are people who were grocers even some years before or after 1813. An additional 57 men and women have been identified as grocers who probably owned real property. Included in this group are people like Don Francisco Larrumbide, who owned a house in 1813 on Calle San Juan. In 1806 a man of that name owned a grocery store near San Juan.

Even employing the larger figure of 73 grocers it is evident that only a minority of the small retail grocers were real property owners. This

Table 13

THE MEXICO CITY GROCERS AS REAL PROPERTY OWNERS*

Quartel & Manzana	Dwelling	Owner	Rent[a] 1813	1796	Change
Q1, M2 m4[b]	casa[a]	Don José Ignacio Sotomayor	852		852
Q2, M5 m12	casa	Lic. Don José Montes de Oca	160	264	-104
Q8, M32 m4	casa	Don José Montes de Oca	30		
Q2, M6 m1	casa casa	Don Domingo Ortiz	700 336	1000	+36
Q3, M12 m13, 14, 15	2 acce-sorías	Don Gabriel Castro	12		
Q4, M15 m5	casa	Don Fernando García Jurado	240		
Q5, M17 m4 Q8, M29 m5	casa casa casa casa casa	Don Juan Monasterio	619.4 330 144 90 246	414 192 144 90 246	+205.4 +138
Q8, M32 m4 Q5, M19 m4	casa casa	Don Antonio Fuentes	72 13		
Q5, M20 m3 m2 m1 m6	corral casa casa hut	Don Manuel Vergara	6 108 24 36	150	-42
Q7, M28	9 acce-sorías	Don Juan José Montes de Oca	81		

Quartel & Manzana	Dwelling	Owner	Rent 1813	1796	Change
Q8, M29 m5	casa	Don Bernardo Zuleta	96	60	+36
Q8, M30 m1	accesoría		48	60	-12
Q8, M30	casa & 5 acce- sorías	Don Matias del Prado	780 294	228	+846
Q1, M4 m3	casa	Don José Rodriguez	192		
Q1, M2 m2	casa casa	Don Joaquín Aldana	600 300	1000	-100
Q4, M14 m8	casa	Don José Zuñiga	240	192	+48
Q8, M29 m3	casa 2 accesorías	Don Clemente Ortega[d]	228 48	96	+132

Notes:
[a]All figures are in pesos. When the owner lived in the dwelling, the figures for rent had to be estimates.
[b]The following abbreviations are employed:
    Q: Quartel Mayor (The city was divided into 8 quarteles mayores and 32 quarteles menores.)
    M: Menor
    m: manzana (block)
[c]The following Spanish terms are employed in the census:
    casa: house
    vivienda: apartment
    accesoría: nook or room at ground floor.
[d]The owner of the house was listed as Clemente Ortega, but they were probably 1 person.

*Source:
Padrón General De Las Casas Que Comprehenden Los Ocho Quarteles Mayores En Que Está Distribuida Esta Capital...(Mexico City, 1903).

coincides with what would be expected of small storekeepers; however, it is interesting that some grocers did own real property, sometimes more than 1 piece of it.

Don Joaquín Aldana, Don Gabriel Castro, and Don Clemente Ortega were grocers in 1781. It has not been possible to document them as grocers in later years. In 1781 Aldana owned 3 grocery stores; thus it is not surprising that he would own 2 houses in the center of the city (cuartel mayor 1, menor 2). The houses were on the same block and in 1813 produced a combined rent of 900 pesos, a substantial sum. (It is possible that Aldana owned a third house in menor 2 that produced a rent of 108 pesos.) Ortega's house produced a rent of 228 pesos, and he also owned 2 accesorías. Castro clearly was not an important income-producing property owner. Don José Montes de Oca and Don Juan José Montes de Oca are the 2 grocers included among the 15 because of their names. The former owned 2 houses producing modest rentals, and the latter owned 9 accesorías, doubtless a business venture.

Although a small group, when considered in guarded terms the 15 grocers are of interest. Their residential holdings, spread throughout the city, in all but 1 of the cuarteles mayores, indicate that several were wealthy when judged by the standards of the general population and by the rest of the property owners. Of those active around the year 1813, 3 grocers owned houses that had rental valuations of more than 500 pesos annually. Four others owned houses that produced more than 200 pesos in rent, still considerable amounts indicative of valuable property.

A caveat is in order: the name José Rodríguez was common. Don José Rodríguez owned a grocery store in 1806 at the corner of Berdeja, and a Don José Rodríguez owned a house on that street in 1813. Almost certainly they were the same people. However, 3 other houses were owned by 1 or more Don José Rodríguezes in 1813. These may not have been owned by the grocer. In fact, it is possible that 3 different Don José Rodríguezes owned grocery stores in 1806, although 2 stores were numbered 182 and 184 and probably owned by the same Rodríguez.

It is interesting that several grocers owned more than 1 dwelling. Don Juan Monasterio owned 5 houses. In 1816 Don Juan Monasterio owned a store in the eighth cuartel mayor on Calle de los Rebeldes. In 1813 Don Juan Monasterio owned a house on Callejón de los Reveldes (possibly the same street as the one of 1816) with a rental of 246 pesos. He owned 2 other houses on a side street within the same block. In 1813 a Don Juan Monasterio owned 2 houses that were more valuable, according to the rents, in another cuartel mayor. With differing addresses and such a simple name as Juan Monasterio, it would be unwise to place too much emphasis on their being the same person. Nonetheless, since the treasury had to collect taxes from multiple-residence owners like Juan Monasterio, one would think that it would have attempted to distinguish between owners of the same name.[4]   However, since the taxes may have been collected at the cuartel mayor or even cuartel menor level, it might not have been necessary to distinguish between owners outside any cuartel. With someone like Don Manual Vergara, the problem is simpler: all of his property was located in the same cuartel menor, the two houses being on *manzanas* 1 and 2.

---

[4]In 1802 Don Juan Monasterio sold a grocery store for the unusually high price of 8,500 pesos (AGNM, Consulados, Tomo 160, "La parte de Don Juan Monasterio con Don Bartolo Alcedo como fiador de su Hermano Don Matias").

Appendix 4
Capitalization
of Some San Juan Pulperías
and Tiendas de Mercería

Table 14 presents the capitalization of 19 San Juan pulperías for the years 1825 through 1865. Six of them were under 1,000 pesos and 3 more were only slightly more highly capitalized. Surprisingly, 3 pulperías were capitalized at more than 5,000 pesos and 3 others at more than 4,000 pesos. The Vicente brothers' pulpería was capitalized at 9,500 pesos, but this was a wholesale-retail operation.

The next highest category of store in San Juan was the tienda de mercería. These were dry goods stores, but their inventories may have been more broadly based than the term mercería suggests. Generally, they were much larger operations than the grocery stores. Of the 9 capitalizations presented in Table 15, not 1 is less than 5,000 pesos.

Table 14

CAPITALIZATION OF SOME SAN JUAN GROCERY STORES*

Name of Owner or Partners	Date	Capitalization	Document
1. José García	1825	95	Will
	1831	957	Will
2. Juan Canobas	1827	500	Will
3. Bernardo López Penales	1828	Approx.	
& José Antonio Forte	or earlier	3,700	Will
4. Juan Cabañas	1830	5,000ª	Will
5. Manuel Marza &			
Juan de la Cruz Sefi	1831	408	Contract
6. Dólores Bárbara to			
Juan Rodriquez	1831	1,247	Contract
7. Antonio Serra & Pedro Salas	1832	6,229	Contract
8. Lucas Hidalgo to			
Juan Antonio de León	1832	1,030	Contract
9. Diego de Aguirre	1833	8,329ᵇ	Will
10. Jayme Julián	1834	300	Will
11. Lamas Vila, Socios, to			
Nicolás Dorado	1845	693ᵇ	Contract
12. Francisco Suárez to			
Goenaga & Molina	1845	2,708	Contract
13. Melchor Alsina to			
Cecilio García	1846	1,211ᵇ	Contract
14. José Benito Dorado &			
Andrés Juan Alvarez	1848	2,507ᶜ	Contract
15. Miguel María Lliteres &			
Francisco Delgado	1851	4,011	Contract
16. Goenaga, Pesquera y Cía.			
to Francisca Feyjoo	1851	1,983ᵇ	Contract
17. Marcelino Vicente &			
Feliciano Vicente	1865	9,500ᵈ	Contract
18. Miguel García	1865	2,430	Sale of Inventory

Notes:
ªThis pulpería also had a warehouse.
ᵇThese figures are in *macuquina* money, worth slightly less than the traditional peso.
ᶜThis store was probably a pulpería.
ᵈThese figures were originally given in *escudos*. In 1865, 1 escudo equalled 2 pesos.

139

*Sources:
All sources are from AGPR, PN. **1.** Caja 446 (1831), ff. 466-68, 496-99 and Caja 495 (1840), folio numbers could not be read; **2.** Caja 442 (1827), ff. 406-8; **3.** Caja 443 (1828), ff. 287-96; **4.** Caja 445 (1830), ff. 54-58; **5.** Caja 446 (1831), ff. 114-15; **6.** Caja 446 (1831), ff. 303-4; **7.** Caja 481 (1832), ff. 632-34; **8.** Caja 480 (1832), ff. 469-71; **9.** Caja 36 (1836), ff. 732-37; **10.** Caja 483 (1834), ff. 282-84; **11.** Caja 450 (1845), f. 101; **12.** Caja 450 (1845), f. 209; **13.** Caja 451 (1846), f. 161; **14.** Caja 453 (1848), folios eaten away. The notary was Joaquín Martínez; **15.** Caja 532 (1853), ff. 2-4; **16.** Caja 531 (1849), ff. 21-23. The contract is dated 1852, but it was placed in a caja marked 1849; **17.** Caja 204 (1865), ff. 1286-92; **18.** Caja 204 (1865), ff. 1156-60.

Table 15

CAPITALIZATION OF SOME SAN JUAN TIENDAS DE MERCERIA*

Name of Owner or Partners	Date	Capitalization	Document
1. Francisco Espar & José Espar	1832	32,884	Contract
2. Ysidoro Labat & José de Aldecoa	1832	16,000	Contract
3. Francisco Espar to Manuel Guillemín	1832	7,490*	Contract
4. Espar brothers to José Goudilo & Dalmán sisters	1841	14,038*	Contract
5. José Pascual López	1847	7,476a	Contract
6. Ramón Carreras & Sebastián Baryuan	1849	8,500	Contract
7. José P. López to Ramón Pelaer	1849	7,396*	Contract
8. Vicente Cañas to Género Pérez de Cortaza	1852	7,296*	Contract
9. Sebastián Baryuan et al.	1852	8,500*	Contract

Note:
*These figures are in macuquina money, worth slightly less than the traditional peso.

*Source:
All sources are from AGPR, PN. **1.** Caja 481 (1832), ff. 304-6; **2.** Caja 480 (1832), ff. 967-68; **3.** Caja 480 (1832), ff. 327-29; **4.** Caja 528 (1841), ff. 213-14; **5.** Caja 452 (1847), ff. 18-19; **6.** Caja 530 (1849), f. 24; **7.** Caja 530 (1849), f. 109; **8.** Caja 251 (1852), ff. 507-8; **9.** Caja 531 (1852), ff. 214-19.

Glossary

The definitions of the following terms vary regionally. They have been defined according to their regional use in this book.

Accesoría	room, recess, or nook in a building often used as a store
Alcabala	sales tax
Alcalde	judicial-administrative official most often in a town council. The *alcalde de cuartel* was roughly a sub-alcalde at the barrio level.
Alhajas	generally cheap, gaudy jewelry
Almacenero	import-export merchant in Mexico City. In many other regions an *almacén* was simply a warehouse, whose owner was also an almacenero. The almacenero of Mexico City had a counterpart in the Buenos Aires *comerciante*. However, the *almacenes* were the principal wholesale suppliers of the pulperías of Buenos Aires.
Apoderado General	legal representative of the pulperos of Mexico City and Puebla and the administrator of their organization. The term also means general legal power.
Arancel	list of legal prices
Bodega	a grocery store in Caracas that sold basically imported items (not only food) at retail. In many places bodegas were simply storage rooms.
Bodeguero	the owner of a bodega
Cacahuatería	in Mexico during the late colonial period, probably similar to pulpería and soon generally considered a pulpería. Today, a store that sells peanuts.

Cajón	shopstall
Cajero	clerk
Cajero Mayor	chief clerk
Canastilla	in Caracas, could be a shopstall or a store located within another store. There were many possible inventories.
Comerciante	in Caracas and Buenos Aires the import-export merchants. In some places, simply merchant.
Dependiente	in stores, generally employee beneath the cajeros. In Mexico City all store employees were sometimes referred to as dependientes.
Depositario	a receiver during bankruptcy proceedings
Fiel Ejecutor	officer of town council charged with immediate supervision of retail stores. His office was the *Fiel Ejecutoria*.
Fuero	special legal jurisdiction
Isleño	someone from the Canary Islands as the term was employed in Caracas
Juicios Verbales	verbal judgments
Licenciado	university graduate or lawyer
Manzana	an urban block
Mercader	in Caracas, wholesaler below comerciante
Padrón	census
Pardo	in many places, such as Caracas and San Juan, free person of color
Prendas	pawns
Procurador	generally legal counsel to a corporate body, such as a town council or court, or simply legal representative
Pulpería	small retail grocery store. Could be a tax, as in Chile.
Pulpero	owner of a pulpería
Real	one-eighth of a silver peso
Regatones	itinerant merchants who habitually intercepted incoming produce and purchased it for resale in the public markets
Regidor	town councilman
Tienda de Mercería	in Caracas and San Juan, dry goods store
Tienda Mestiza	in Puebla, and probably Mexico City, principal wholesale supplier to pulperías. They sold other items, including, generally, dry goods.
Tlaco	one-eight of a real
Vinatería	wine store in Mexico
Vinatero	owner of a wine store in Mexico
Visita	official supervisory visit

Bibliography

In this bibliography I have attempted to indicate the sources for the book without repeating the notes. Thus I have cited the various archival branches without listing the specific legajos or bundles, etc., except in the case of the Spanish American notary records. Here I felt the reader might require more specific information.

I. PRIMARY SOURCES

A. Archives

Puebla

1. *Archivo Judicial de Puebla* (AJP)
   Fondos Antiguos (FA)
2. *Archivo del Ayuntamiento de Puebla* (AAP)
   In addition to the minutes, *Actas*, this archive holds the various town council rulings and grocer petitions.
3. *Archivo de Notarías de Puebla* (ANP)

Notary Number*	Year
#2	1799, 1806, 1816
#4	1802, 1803
#5	1790-95, 1800, 1806, 1807
#6	1806, 1809, 1810, 1811, 1812
#7	1806, 1814, 1827

   *Often several notaries functioned during a given year under the same notary number.

Mexico City

1. *Archivo General de la Nación* (AGNM)
   Consulado
   Indiferente General (IG)
   Indiferente de Guerra (IGG)
   Padrones
   Real Hacienda
2. *Archivo del Ex-Ayuntamiento de la Ciudad de México* (AAM)
   In this rich archive are documents dealing with town council
   supervision of storekeepers, store censuses, and related matters, such
   as education.
3. *Archivo Histórico de Hacienda* (AHH)
   Consulados
4. *Archivo Judicial del Tribunal Superior de Justicia del Distrito
   Federal* (Tribunales)
   Papeles Sueltos
   Juzgado de Letras (in Papeles Sueltos)
5. *Archivo de Notarías del Distrito Federal* (ANM)
   For Mexico City it is important to know the name of the notary.

Notary	Year
Adán	1772-74, 1773, 1778-80, 1784-86, 1784-87, 1785, 1787, 1787-89, 1789, 1792
Calapiz	1794
Madariaga	1818
Morales	1775

Caracas

1. *Archivo General de la Nación* (AGNV)
   Capitanía General (Diversos, Reales Cédulas)
   Real Hacienda (La Colonia)
   Intendencia y Real Hacienda
2. *Archivo del Consejo Municipal* (ACM)
   Actas del Cabildo
   Capitulares
   Propios
   Visitas
3. *Registro Principal* (RP)
   The notaries are in Escribanías and Protocolos.

Notary	Year
Alvarado (Registrador)	1838, 1839
Aramburu	1797, 1800, 1802, 1803, 1807, 1813
Arocha	1800
Ascanio	1805, 1810
José Domingo Barcena	1797, 1800
Juan Domingo Barcena	1803
Juan Manuel Barcena	1825
Castillo	1813, 1817
Cires	1803
Cobran	1802
Juan Pablo Correa	1814, 1815
A. Hernández	1807
F. Hernández Guerra	1819, 1835
Jimenes	1813
Antonio Juan Ochoa	1830
Ravelo	1810
Santana	1807
Antonio Juan Texera	1803, 1807
Miguel Texera	1817, 1820
Therreros	1765
Tirado	1803, 1816
Urbina	1813, 1817

San Juan

1. *Archivo General de Puerto Rico* (AGPR)
   Documentos de los Gobernadores de Puerto Rico (DGPR)
   Censos y Riquezas, 1801-20
   Political & Civil Affairs, Visitas, 1818-24
   Protocolos Notariales (PN)
   The following are all for San Juan: Cajas: 36 (1833); 204 (1865); 251 (1852); 442 (1827); 443 (1828); 445 (1830); 446 (1831); 450 (1845); 451 (1846); 452 (1846); 453 (1848); 474 (1824); 480 (1832); 481 (1832); 483 (1834); 495 (1840); 528 (1841); 530 (1849); 531 (1849 & 1852); 532 (1853).

Buenos Aires

1. *Archivo General de la Nación* (AGNA)
   División Gobierno, Sección Gobierno, Sala IX
   Hacienda, Sala X
   Interior, Sala X
   Pulperías, Sala IX
   Tribunales (Comerciales)

Registro de Escribano (in Escribanías)
#3 (?), 1789
#4 (Iranzuaga), 1813-15
#5 (Boyso), 1812-15
#6 (Echaburu), 1788; (Agrelo), 1806

New York City

1. *Historical Documents Collection* (HDC), Queens College
   Inventories of Estates
   Wills (in Libers)
   Minutes of the Mayor's Court (MC)
   New York City Jury Lists
   Tax Assessment Lists
2. *Municipal Archives* (MA)
   Market Committee (City Clerk Filed Papers)
   Police Committee (City Clerk Filed Papers)
3. *Office of the City Register* (OCR)
   Conveyances of Deeds
4. *New York Historical Society* (NYHS)
   Manuscript Room
5. *New York Public Library* (NYPL)
   Manuscript Division

B. Printed Documents and Contemporary Works

Actas del cabildo de Caracas, 1810-1811. vol. 1. Caracas, 1971.
Acuerdos del extinguido cabildo de Buenos Aires. 47 vols, Serie 3. Buenos Aires, 1907-34.
Almanaque político y de comercio de la ciudad de Buenos Aires para el año de 1826. Buenos Aires, 1968.

Bullock, W. *Six Months' Residence and Travels in Mexico.* 1824. Port Washington, NY, 1971.

Calderón de la Barca, Fanny. *Life in Mexico.* Edited by Howard T. Fisher and Marian Hall Fisher. New York, 1970.
Código de Comercio. In *Legislación Ultramarina: Concordada y Anotada,* vol. 5. D. Joaquín Rodríguez San Pedro. Madrid, 1866.

Defoe, Daniel. *The Complete English Tradesman.* 2 vols. 1726. New York, 1970.
Depons, F. *Travels in South America.* 2 vols. London, 1807. Reprint. 1970.

Facultad de Filosofía y Letras, Universidad de Buenos Aires. *Documentos para la historia argentina: tomo XI, territorio y población: padrón de la ciudad de Buenos Aires (1778).* Buenos Aires, 1919.

Facultad de Filosofía, Universidad de Buenos Aires. *Documentos para la historia del Virreinato del Río de la Plata.* 3 vols. Buenos Aires, 1912-13.

Fonseca, Fabián de and Urrutia, Carlos de. *Historia general de real hacienda.* 6 vols. Mexico City, 1945-53.

Galván Rivera, Mariano, compilador. *Guía de forasteros de México para el año de 1829.* México, 1829.

García Cubas, Antonio. *El libro de mis recuerdos.* Mexico City, 1945.

Longworth's American Almanac, New York Register, And City-Directory. New York, by year.

Lorenzot, Francisco del Barrio, compilador. *Ordenanzas de gremios de la Nueva España.* Mexico City, 1920.

Minutes of the Common Council of the City of New York, 1784-1831. 19 vols. New York, 1917.

Ordenanzas de la ilustre Universidad, y Casa de contratación de la m. n. y m. l. villa de Bilbao. Madrid, many editions.

Padrón general de las casas que comprehenden los ocho quarteles mayores en que está distribuida esta capital...1813. Mexico City, 1903.

Prieto, Guillermo. *Ocho días en Puebla.* Mexico City, 1944.

Recopilación de leyes de los reynos de las Indias. 3 vols. Madrid, 1943.

Silva Herzog, Jesús, ed. *Relaciones estadísdicas de Nueva España de principios del siglo XIX. Archivo Histórico de Hacienda,* vol. 3. Mexico City, 1944.

Un Inglés. *Cinco años en Buenos Aires, 1820-1825.* 2nd ed. Buenos Aires, 1962.

Vidal, Esq., E.E. *Picturesque Illustrations of Buenos Ayres and Monte Video...* Reprinted in English from the original London 1820 edition. Buenos Aires, 1943.

Villa Sánchez, Fray Juan. *Puebla: sagrada y profana.* Puebla, 1835. Reprint. Mexico City, 1962.

Wilde, José Antonio. *Buenos Aires desde setenta años atrás.* 2nd ed. Buenos Aires, 1948.

C. Newspapers

Diario de México. 1807.
Gaceta de Buenos Aires. 1819. This is from the reimpresión fascimilar. Buenos Aires, 1914.
New York Evening Post. 1810.

II. SECONDARY SOURCES

Alvarez, Mercedes M. *Comercio y comerciantes.* Caracas, 1963.
_____. *El Tribunal del real consulado de Caracas.* 2 vols. Caracas, 1967.
Andrews, George R. *The Afro-Argentines of Buenos Aires, 1800-1900.* Madison, 1980.
Archer, Criston I. *The Army in Bourbon Mexico, 1760-1810.* Albuquerque, 1977.
Arrom, Silvia M. "Marriage Patterns in Mexico City, 1811." *Journal of Family History* 3, no. 4 (winter 1978): 376-91.
Atherton, Lewis E. *The Southern Country Store, 1800-1860.* Baton Rouge, 1949.
_____. *The Frontier Merchant in Mid-America.* Columbia, MO, 1971.

Bauer, Arnold J. "The Church in the Economy of Spanish America: *Censos* and *Depósitos* in the Eighteenth and Nineteenth Centuries." *Hispanic American Historical Review* 63, no. 4 (Nov. 1983): 707-33.
Bayle, Constantino. *Los cabildos seculares en la America Española.* Madrid, 1952.
Bazant, Jan. "Evolución de la industria textil poblana (1544-1845)." *Historia Mexicana* 13, no. 4 (April-June 1964): 473-516.
_____. "Industria algodonera poblana de 1800-1843 en números." *Historia Mexicana* 14, no. 1 (July-Sept. 1964): 131-43.
Beard, Miriam. *A History of Business.* 2 vols. pb. Ann Arbor, 1963.
Boletín Historico de Puerto Rico. 13: 317-19.
Bossio, Jorge A. *Historia de las pulperías.* Buenos Aires, 1972.
Bowser, Frederick P. *The African Slave in Colonial Peru, 1684-1750.* Stanford, 1974.
Boyd-Bowman, Peter. "Two Country Stores in XVIIth Century Mexico." *The Americas* 28, no. 3 (Jan. 1972): 237-51.
Brading, D.A. *Miners and Merchants in Bourbon Mexico, 1750-1821.* Cambridge, Eng., 1971.
Braudel, Fernand. *The Wheels of Commerce. Civilization and Capitalism, 15th-18th Century,* vol. 2. tr. New York, 1982.

Carson, Gerald. *The Old Country Store.* pb. New York, 1965.
Castilleja, Aida. "Asignación del espacio urbano: el gremio de los panaderos, 1770-1793." In *Ciudad de Mexico: ensayo de construcción de una historia.* Coordinated by Alejandra Moreno Toscano. Mexico City, 1978.
Costeloe, Michael P. *Church Wealth in Mexico: A Study of the 'Juzgado de Capellanías' in the Archbishopric of Mexico 1800-1856.* Cambridge, Eng., 1967.
Couturier, Edith. "Micaela Angela Carrillo: Widow and Pulque Dealer." In *Struggle & Survival in Colonial America.* Edited by David G. Sweet and Gary B. Nash, pp. 362-75. Berkeley, 1981.

Davies, Keith A. "Tendencias demográficas urbanas durante el siglo XIX en México." *Historia Mexicana* 21, no. 3 (Jan.-March 1972): 481-524.
Davis, Dorothy. *A History of Shopping.* Toronto, 1966.
Dawley, Alan. *Class and Community: The Industrial Revolution in Lynn.* Cambridge, MA, 1976.

Flores Caballero, Romeo. *La contrarevolución en la independencia.* Mexico City, 1969.
Flory, Rae and Smith, David Grant. "Bahian Merchants and Planters in the Seventeenth and Early Eighteenth Centuries." *Hispanic American Historical Review* 58, no. 4 (Nov. 1978): 571-94.

Gade, Daniel W. "The Latin American Central Plaza as a Functional Space." In *Latin America: Search for Geographic Explanations.* Edited by Robert J. Tata, pp. 16-23. Chapel Hill, 1976.
García Belsunce, César A., director. *Buenos Aires: su gente, 1800-1830.* Buenos Aires, 1976.
Góngora, Mario. "Urban Social Stratification in Colonial Chile." *Hispanic American Historical Review* 55, no. 3 (Aug. 1975): 421-48.
González Angulo, Jorge. "Establecimientos comerciales, 1816." In *Investigaciones sobre la historia de la ciudad de Mexico, 1.* Coordinated by Alejandra Moreno Toscano. Mexico City, 1974.
Greenow, Linda. *Credit and Socioeconomic Change in Colonial Mexico: Loans and Mortgages in Guadalajara, 1720-1820.* Dellplain Latin American Studies, no. 12. Boulder, 1983.

Haring, C.H. *The Spanish Empire in America.* New York, A Harbinger Book, 1963.
Hobsbawn, E.J. "Class Consciousness in History." In *Aspects of History and Class Consciousness.* Edited by István Mészaros, pp. 5-21. New York, 1972.
Horvitz Vásquez, María Eugenia. "Ensayo sobre el crédito en Chile colonial." Memoria De Prueba, Santiago, 1966.

150

Israel, J.I. *Race, Class and Politics in Colonial Mexico, 1610-1670.* Oxford, 1975.

Johnson, Lyman L. "The Artisans of Buenos Aires during the Viceroyalty, 1776-1810." Ph.D. dissertation, The University of Connecticut, 1974.
Johnson, Lyman L. and Socolow, Susan Midgen. "Population and Space in Eighteenth Century Buenos Aires." In *Social Fabric and Spatial Structure in Colonial Latin America.* Edited by David Robinson. Ann Arbor, 1979.

Kicza, John E. "The Pulque Trade of Late Colonial Mexico City." *The Americas* 37, no. 2 (Oct. 1980): 193-221.
_____. *Colonial Entrepreneurs: Families and Business in Bourbon Mexico City.* Albuquerque, 1983.
Kinsbruner, Jay. "The Pulperos of Caracas and San Juan during the First Half of the Nineteenth Century." *Latin American Research Review* 13, no. 1 (1978): 65-85.
Kroos, Herman, E. and Gilbert, Charles. *American Business History.* pb. Englewood Cliffs, 1972.

Laslett, Peter, ed. *Household and Family in Past Time.* pb. Cambridge, Eng., 1974.
Lavrin, Asunción, ed. *Latin American Women: Historical Perspectives.* Westport, CT, 1978.
Leicht, Dr. Hugo. *Las calles de Puebla: estudio histórico.* Puebla, 1934.
Liehr, Reinhard. *Ayuntamiento y oligarquía en Puebla, 1787-1810.* 2 vols. tr. Mexico City, 1976.
Lockhart, James. *Spanish Peru, 1532-1560.* pb. Madison, 1968.
Lombardi, John V. *People and Places in Colonial Venezuela.* Bloomington, 1976.

MacLachlan, Colin M. and Rodriguez O., Jaime E. *The Forging of the Cosmic Race.* Berkeley, 1980.
McParland, Eugene. "The Socio-Economic Importance of the Colonial Tavern in New York during the British Period: 1664-1776." M.A. thesis, Queens College, 1970.
Martínez-Alier, Verena. *Marriage, Class and Colour in Nineteenth-Century Cuba.* Cambridge, Eng., 1974.
Medina, José Toribio, ed. *Cosas de la colonia.* Santiago, 1952.
Morales, Carmen. "Propiedad urbana de las corporaciones religiosas, 1860." In *Investigaciones sobre la historia de la ciudad de Mexico, 1.* Coordinated by Alejandra Moreno Toscano. Mexico City, 1974.
Moreno, José Luis. "La estructura social y demográfica de la ciudad de Buenos Aires en el año 1778." *Anuario del Instituto de*

Investigaciones Históricas, pp. 151-70. Universidad del Litoral, Rosario, Arg., 1965.

Mörner, Magnus. *La distribución de ingresos en un distrito Andino en los años 1830*. Research Paper Series, no. 1. Institute of Latin American Studies, Stockholm, Jan. 1977.

Muñoz, Miguel L. *Tlacos y pilones: la moneda del pueblo de México*. Mexico City, 1976.

Pomerantz, Sidney I. *New York: An American City, 1783-1803*. New York, 1938.

Ricardo, Irma De-Solá. *Contribución al estudio de los planos de Caracas, la ciudad y la provincia, 1567-1967*. Caracas, 1967.

Rock, Howard B. *Artisans of the New Republic: The Tradesmen of New York City in the Age of Jefferson*. New York, 1979.

Russell-Wood, A.J.R. "Colonial Brazil." In *Neither Slave Nor Free*. Edited by David W. Cohen and Jack P. Greene. Baltimore, 1972.

Sánchez de Tagle, Rosa María. "Elements for the Analysis of the Internal Structure of Mexico City: A Typology of Dwellings." *Latin American Research Review* 10, no. 2 (summer 1975): 121-22.

Scobie, James R. *Revolution on the Pampas: A Social History of Argentine Wheat, 1860-1910*. Austin, 1964.

Shaw, Frederick John, Jr. "Poverty and Politics in Mexico City, 1824-1854." Ph.D. dissertation, The University of Florida, 1975.

Slatta, Richard W. "Pulperías and Contraband Capitalism in Nineteenth-Century Buenos Aires Province." *The Americas* 38, no. 3 (Jan. 1982): 347-62.

Smith, Robert S. "Sales Taxes in New Spain, 1575-1770." *Hispanic American Historical Review* 28, no. 1 (Feb. 1948): 2-37.

Socolow, Susan M. *The Merchants of Buenos Aires, 1778-1810*. Cambridge, Eng., 1978.

Super, John C. "Bread and the Provisioning of Mexico City in the Late Eighteenth Century." *Jahrbuch für die Geschichte von Staat, Wirtschaft und Gesellschaft Lateinamerikas* 19 (1982): 159-82.

Swann, Michael M. *Tierra Adentro: Settlement and Society in Colonial Durango*. Dellplain Latin American Studies, no. 10. Boulder, 1982.

Szaszdi, Adam. "Credit--Without Banking--in Early Nineteenth Century Puerto Rico." *The Americas* 19, no. 2 (Oct. 1962): 149-71.

Tanck Estrada, Dorothy. *La educación ilustrada (1786-1836)*. Mexico City, 1977.

Tax, Sol. *Penny Capitalism: A Guatemalan Indian Economy*. 2nd ed. New York, 1972.

Tjarks, Germán O.E. *El consulado de Buenos Aires y sus proyecciones en la historia*. 2 vols. Buenos Aires, 1962?.

Twinam, Ann. "Miners, Merchants, and Farmers: The Roots of Entrepreneurship in Antioquia." Ph.D. dissertation, Yale University, 1976.

Uslar Pietri, Juan. *Historia de la rebelión popular de 1814*. Caracas, 1972.

Vicens Vives, Jaime. *An Economic History of Spain*. tr. Princeton, 1969.

Waldron, Kathleen. "A Social History of a Primate City: The Case of Caracas, 1750-1810." Ph.D. dissertation, Indiana University, 1977.

Wedovoy, Enrique. *La evolución económica rioplatense a fines del siglo XVIII y principios del siglo XIX a la luz de la historia del seguro*. La Plata, 1962.

Index

154

Morales, Don Rafael, 44
Moreno y Calderón, Don José,
    95-96
Morín, Pedro, 125
Moya, Don José Reymundo de,
    2-3, 35n.30, 59
Mozos, 75-76, 82n.36
Muñoz, Don Matías, 43

Negrón, Don Eugenio, 66
New York City, 100-101; New
    York and Spanish American
    grocers compared, 101-5
Nieto, Don Francisco, 43
Nuñes, Don Miguel, 125-27

Obligado, Don Antonio, 93-94
Ocaña, Don Rafael, 44
Ochoa, Don Sebastián, 42
Ordenanza (tax), 4n.8, 12n.35,
    52-53n.82
Ordenanzas para...los tenderos de
    Pulperia...(1757), 56, 70, 77-
    83
Oropeza, Don Manuel, 43
Oropeza, Don Mariano, 42
Orruño, Don Manuel, 48
Ortega, Don Clemente, 51n.79,
    133-34
Ortega, Don Juan, 44
Ortiz, Don Domingo, 132
Ortiz, Don José, 42
Ortuño, Don Nicolas, 58, 71
Otero, Don Gregorio, 42

Padrón Sánchez, Don Juan, 66
Pardo, 122-23
Paredes, Don Ygnacio, 44
Parodi, Don Santiago, 64, 88n.63
Partners, 52-54, 125-26, 129n.1
Pastor, Don Emeterio, 44
Pawnbroking: Mexico City, 56,
    58-61; Puebla, 56, 60
Pedraza, Don José, 108, 110
Pellicer, Don Francisco, 126-27
Pellicer, Don Juan, 127
Peña, Manuel, 125

Pensión (tax), 10n.28, 10-11n.32,
    14-15n.49, 55, 80. See also
    Alcabala
Pérez, Don Pedro Manuel, 124
Pérez, Don Salvador, 126
Pérez Calanche, Don Ramón, 66
Pérez Forte, Don Juan, 66
Pérez Fuentes, Don Domingo, 66
Pérez García, Don Juan, 66, 129-
    30n.2
Pérez Guzmán, Don Antonio,
    126-27
Pino, Don José Antonio, 124
Pinzón, Don José, 42
Pomar, Don José, 46
Ponce, Don Francisco, 66
Ponce, Paula, 125
Porras, Doña María Petronila,
    125-27
Prado, Don Matías del Prado,
    133
Profits. See Grocers
Puebla, 3-4, 9-11, 14, 18-23, 29-
    31, 34, 40-43, 46, 52, 55-56,
    60, 75-79
Pulperas. See Female grocers
Pulperías. See Grocery stores
Pulperos. See Grocers
Pulque (and pulquerías), 50

Querní, Doña María, 42
Quijano, Don Ygnacio, 44

Racial restrictions, 82, 88n.62,
    96, 98
Ramires, Don Juan José, 66-67
Ramírez, Don José María, 71
Ramiro, Don Félix, 42
Ramos, Don Vicente, 125
Ranchos, 24-25, 61, 66
Regatones, 5n.10, 78
Reglamento...de Tiendas de
    Pulpería (1810), 56, 82-83
Reveson, Don Luis, 125
Reyes, Don Bartolomé, 66, 129-
    30n.2
Reyes, Don Pedro, 125n.17

Dellplain Latin American Studies
Published by Westview Press